SOSA

AN AUTOBIOGRAPHY

SOSA

AN AUTOBIOGRAPHY

Sammy Sosa
with Marcos Bretón

WARNER BOOKS

A Time Warner Company

Warner Books, Inc., 1271 Avenue of the Americas, New York, NY 10020
Visit our Web site at www.twbookmark.com

 A Time Warner Company

Printed in the United States of America
First Printing: May 2000
10 9 8 7 6 5 4 3 2 1

ISBN: 0-446-52735-1
LCCN: 00-101464

I dedicate this book to my love of God, as a way of showing thanks for my life, for my ability, and for teaching me humility. To my beloved mother, to whom I dedicated 66 kisses in 1998. To my wife, for her constant faith and patience and for blessing me with our four children—my fountain of inspiration. To my brothers, sisters, and family, who have always been at my side. To my friend and brother Domingo Dauhajre, his wife Yanilka, and their beautiful family. To my agent, Adam Katz, and to Mr. and Mrs. Bill Chase. To everyone at the Chicago Cubs, Larry Himes, Hector Peguero, Amado Dinzey, and Omar Minaya. And to my fans everywhere.

—Sammy Sosa

To my wife, Jeannie.
There is no word in English or Spanish to describe how much she means to me.

—Marcos Bretón

Contents

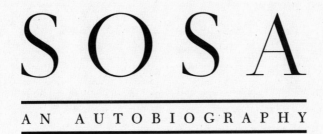

SOSA

AN AUTOBIOGRAPHY

Introduction

Who is Sammy Sosa?

How did he become an international celebrity? How did he rise to the top of the heap in the post-Jordan sports world—not only in Chicago but nationwide?

It's amazing to consider that, seemingly overnight, Sosa has transcended sports. One moment he is lighting the national Christmas tree with President Clinton and being singled out and applauded heartily at a State of the Union address. The next, there is Sosa on countless television commercials, extolling the virtues of his native Dominican Republic.

When the prime minister of Japan came to Chicago, who was the first person he wanted to meet?

Sosa.

Asked early in 2000 about his biggest regret, Texas Governor and presidential hopeful George W. Bush—formerly managing general partner of the Texas Rangers—said, "My biggest mistake was trading Sammy Sosa."

Incredible—particularly when you consider that as recently as the spring of 1998, Sammy Sosa was only somewhat known in the baseball world. Few outside the sport had ever heard of him and, to be truthful, he was kind of an enigma to his peers.

His detractors called him "Sammy So-So." There were questions about his abilities. He was considered a middle-tier player who never scored well on baseball's fame indicator: all-star votes. In fact in 1996, Sosa was leading the National League in home runs at the all-star break, yet he didn't inspire enough respect to make the team as a reserve. He stayed home.

From 1993 to 1997, Sosa quietly put up big numbers, but even his home-run and stolen-base totals were questioned and discounted the few times the national spotlight shined his way.

"Numbers? Sure, Sosa had them. So did World B. Free, Eric Dickerson and Imelda Marcos," wrote Tom Verducci of *Sports Illustrated*.

> Partly a creation of Wrigley Field's cozy dimensions, the notoriously undisciplined Sosa through his first nine seasons racked up nearly as many strikeouts as hits. . . . His [1997 season] was probably the worst year ever by anyone with 36 dingers and 119 RBIs. Behind that impressive-looking façade, Sosa hit poorly with runners in scoring position (.246), was virtually an automatic out on any two-strike count (.159), whiffed more than anyone else in the National League . . .

With this kind of press, it's no wonder that Sosa surprised everyone when it was he—and not Ken Griffey, Jr.—who took his place alongside Mark McGwire in the great home-run chase of 1998.

As the home runs started flying, so did the questions.

When Sosa became the first player in the century-old history of our national pastime to hit 20 home runs in one month—June 1998—the question was: How did he do that?

When Sosa stayed with McGwire into August, it was: When will Sammy fall off the pace?

When McGwire surpassed Roger Maris's single-season mark of 61 home runs and then Sosa pulled even with him, people wondered: How is Sammy handling everything so well?

And finally, when Sosa finished his remarkable year with 66 home runs—four shy of McGwire's total—with his Cubs securing a playoff spot and the MVP trophy awarded to him, the question was: How did Sammy develop into such a *superstar*?

In Sosa's case, that overused word fit not only because of what he did on the field but the way he carried himself off of it. We ask a lot of our superstars as we enter the twenty-first century: they must be great, they must photograph well, they must be gracious and say the right things, and they must steer clear of trouble.

Dennis Rodman was amusing for a while, but that "bad-boy" act got old fast, and it sure didn't sell beyond a niche audience.

Sosa does. He is a phenomenon because he did something great in 1998 and did it again in 1999 by hitting 63 home runs—that's 129 home runs in two seasons. And all the while he seemed to have fun. He was accessible to the masses buying the tickets, behaving as we all hoped our stars would. The examples are like a highlight reel, a textbook in how athletes should interact with the fans who make them rich beyond belief: Remember when Sosa ran in from right field to embrace McGwire after Big Mac broke the record? Or all those famous blown kisses to his mama after each home run? Or that ever-present smile?

After a while, Sosa became a living antidote to baseball's recent poisonous past, in particular the 1994 baseball strike that canceled the World Series. And in the process, Sosa developed an appeal that extended beyond his sport. Believe me, I've seen it.

Last November I was waiting for Sosa and his entourage at a trendy Miami restaurant, a dazzling place known mostly for playing host to Hollywood stars, movie moguls, and music-industry titans. It was a gorgeous Saturday night in South

Beach, and the place was jammed with beautiful, wealthy people who don't impress easily. Yet when Sosa strode in wearing an exquisite blue suit, he stopped traffic. People who had been waiting all night to get in could only watch as Sosa, his manager, Domingo Dauhajre, two brothers, and a couple of security guards were immediately shown to a table in the middle of the dining room.

There would be no private rooms for Sosa. He wanted to be around people. With blaring techno music as a background, a steady stream of well-wishers began making their way over. Patrons sitting at the bar, so cool and detached before Sosa arrived, were suddenly waving at him like schoolkids on a day trip to Wrigley Field. At one point an artist brought over some god-awful-looking painting and wouldn't leave until he gave it to Sammy.

Amazingly, Sosa motioned his people to let him through. Suddenly a television camera appeared, and the restaurant owner came over to ask if Sosa would pose for a picture and endorse the place. The answer was no. Why? Because Sammy owns his own restaurant in Chicago and can't go around endorsing other places. Business is business.

Just the typical American fascination with celebrities? No way.

Think about it: how many foreign-born athletes have Americans truly loved and cheered for as much as Sosa is today?

Hakeem Olajuwon is respected and admired. But loved? Not outside of Houston. Every four years some foreign-born Olympian rouses our momentary interest but then fades and is forgotten. Pele generated some headlines in the 1970s and was admired among a certain audience—but at least in this country, his fame was nothing like that of "Slammin' Sammy."

Even the late, great Roberto Clemente—the greatest Latin

baseball player of all time—never enjoyed the fame and respect that came only after he died in a plane crash following the 1972 baseball season.

It must be said that before Sosa, Americans—in our national belief that we are the best—had never truly embraced a great athlete from another country and welcomed him into the highest levels of fame and stardom. That Sosa changed that about us is not insignificant.

Plainly stated, Sosa sells in Peoria and everywhere else. The largest marketing firms in America today view Sosa's name as a valuable brand label. Invitations to every event possible pour into his administrative offices in Chicago and the Dominican Republic. Everyone wants a piece of him—he is baseball's cover boy.

And he is Dominican and he is black. That's progress in my book, because I can remember a time just a few years ago when the best Latin players in the major leagues felt like third-class citizens in America's game.

But it's a brave new world now.

Make no mistake, many of Sosa's admirers follow him for reasons that have nothing to do with baseball.

I remember being at the UNITY Conference in Seattle in July of 1999—the largest gathering ever of Latino, African American, Asian American, and Native American journalists. A Native American leader shook my hand and said, "I love Sammy Sosa. In 1998, when he was going after the record, all of our people were with him."

Her meaning was this: Sosa's great achievements gave inspiration to people outside the mainstream, people who took heart when they saw Americans embracing someone from another culture.

Add to that his appeal to the mainstream, and you have a

star who just moved into a $5 million home, who is revered in his own country as an icon, and is in his prime at the age of thirty-one.

Like most overnight sensations, Sosa had earned his stripes in life when fame came calling—he took his knocks, paid his dues, made his mistakes, and learned from them.

He was called a "selfish" player by some in the press and by some teammates. Whether fair or unfair, that reputation followed Sosa through eight-plus seasons in the big leagues by the time 1998 rolled around. At that point Sosa was still casting off the tag as the consummate "potential" player of the 1990s, the guy who inspired the type of awed predictions so endemic to the game. Isn't the eternal hope of spring part of the lore of our national pastime? Doesn't April in America mean the annual discovery of the "next great . . . "?

People had been laying those expectations on Sosa for years. In Chicago in the 1990s, summertime always meant two things: bleacher bums at Wrigley and a column by hall-of-fame writer Jerome Holtzman claiming that Sosa was right on the verge of stardom.

The acclaim started early. Sosa was tagged for greatness when he was still a teenager, when he was only a few years removed from devastating poverty, when he was barely learning the game of baseball, let alone the English language.

He reached the big leagues at the tender age of twenty, in the early summer of 1989. He had a big smile, a strong arm, a wild swing, and a reckless attitude that, mixed together with flashes of brilliance, added up to a new "phenom."

But the acclaim was fleeting, and the potential was slow in arriving completely. Then, judging by his newspaper clippings, Sosa suffered the flip side of springtime hopefulness—the hot glare of summertime expectations unfulfilled.

That's when the Sammy "So-So" tag took hold completely. It wasn't that he didn't do great things. In 1993 he became only the tenth player in National League history to hit more than 30 home runs and steal more than 30 bases in one season. In 1995 he did it again, and he also led the league in games, was an all-star, and was second in the NL in homers and RBI, with 36 and 119 respectively.

But he struck out—a lot. He fanned 135 times in 1993 and 134 times each in 1995 and 1996. Sosa's first truly dominant season—1995—came the first year after baseball's paralyzing strike, which kept angry fans away as Sosa was coming into his own.

Things weren't much better for the game in 1996, but Sosa was continuing to improve and making great strides—though with little fanfare. That was the year the Atlanta Braves manager, Bobby Cox, left Sosa off the All-Star Game roster, even though Sosa was leading the National League in home runs midway through the season.

Sosa's low profile back then was part of a larger story: the then-unrealized dominance and acceptance of Latin players in major league baseball.

Latin players have a long history in the game, and they were doing great things in the years just before and after the 1994 strike. Juan Gonzalez, Sosa's old minor league teammate, hit 43 home runs in 1992 and 46 in 1993. And in 1996 Gonzalez was the American League's MVP—not the last time he would win that honor. Robby Alomar, another Puerto Rican like Gonzalez, became the best second baseman in baseball while helping his Toronto Blue Jays win two straight world championships, in 1992 and 1993.

Other Latin players, like Rafael Palmeiro and Ivan Rodriguez of the Texas Rangers, and Andres Galarraga, then of the Colorado Rockies, put up great numbers. But they were all pretty much in the same boat as Sosa. They were respected for their talents and paid handsomely for their services, but their names hardly resonated outside their respective cities. In 1993 Juan Gonzalez told me: "With my numbers, if I were an American, my name would be heard everywhere."

Language barriers had much to do with it. Baseball, more than any other sport, has been mythologized through the written word; it is a game dependent on the description, the quote.

For players who don't dominate English the way they do the outside corner of the plate, it means little space in the news columns, little demand to do commercials, less TV time, limited exposure.

Clemente used to rail at reporters and columnists in the 1960s and early 1970s, denouncing their muted, sometimes hostile reactions to his demands to be recognized for who he was—one of the great players of his or any generation. And after Clemente's death, the plight of Latin players in America's game stayed mostly within baseball's fraternity of foreigners.

That still held true as Sosa—the NL Player of July for hitting .358 in 26 games, with 22 runs scored, 10 homers, and 29 RBI—sat at home watching the 1996 All-Star Game on TV. And when he returned to the field after his all-star snub, Sosa picked up where he left off and was headed for a monster year. With six weeks to go in the season, Sosa was leading the National League with 40 home runs.

Fifty home runs or more was a realistic goal and would have put him on a whole other level of fame and respect; that many home runs in a season has always been a mark associated with greatness. Hell, Hank Aaron—the greatest home run hitter of all time—never hit 50 in one year.

But on August 20, 1996, Sosa was hit on the hand by a pitch thrown by Florida's Mark Hutton. It broke a bone, and Sosa was done for the year.

Denied this opportunity to join the game's elite, Sosa was

nonetheless building toward something—in 1997, after four consecutive solid years, the Cubs rewarded him with a four-year, $42.5 million contract. That move was not accepted well by fans and the press, who conceded that Sosa had talent—he hit 36 home runs and had 119 RBI in 1997—but were put off by other aspects of his game.

Toward the end of the 1997 season, Sosa was dressed down by his manager amid accusations that he was putting his own stats before the team's needs. Stung by the criticism, Sosa arrived in 1998 ready to go. He had his money, he had the experience, he knew something about the downside of press coverage, and he had the discipline of someone willing to learn from his experiences. Coupled with the incredible talent he never lost faith in, Sosa exploded.

America had never seen anything like him, and the nation was caught unprepared when the homers started flying out of Wrigley. But more important than us being ready for Sosa was that Sosa had become ready for us. And by the time we had caught on that something special was happening on Waveland Avenue, Sosa was waiting for us with that smile of his.

Then Sosa showed he had the one quality all superstars need: magic.

For me, one night stands out. On September 16, 1998, I was in San Diego, covering the ongoing Sosa phenomenon for my newspaper, the *Sacramento Bee*. A few days before, Sosa had shocked the nation by pulling even with McGwire at 62 home runs, just after McGwire had broken Roger Maris's record.

Didn't we all think the race was over after McGwire had hugged Roger Maris's kids?

But on this night, before a capacity crowd at Qualcomm Stadium, Sosa was trailing McGwire again, 63 to 62. This was the third of four games between the Cubs and Padres. Each Sosa at-bat moved the thousands at Qualcomm to stand and scream just like baseball crowds do in the movies. And by the time he came up in the eighth inning on that evening in September, Sosa had played well and hit well, though he hadn't done what everyone wanted—hit a home run.

This particular game was crucial to Chicago because they were fighting for a playoff spot. And the Padres also wanted to win badly because they were in first place and vying for home-field advantage in the playoffs.

To add to the tension, Sosa came up in the eighth with the bases loaded and the Cubs down 3–2.

The 50,000-plus crowd was on its feet again, screaming so loudly it seemed impossible to concentrate. Each pitch drew a firestorm of flashbulbs from all over the stadium. Each swing and miss brought an amazing unified groan.

And then Brian Boehringer of the Padres hung one out over the plate.

I'll never forget that moment. I was standing in the left-field bleachers, and I saw Sosa follow through against a backdrop of flashing lights. When he connected, the thousands of people in the sections in front of me seemed to move as one. Then the screams of the crowd grew louder and louder as the ball sailed toward the bleachers.

And before I knew it, the ball was soaring over me, over all the people in the lower pavilion and into the second deck— 434 feet from home plate.

A grand slam. Home run number 63.

Even though Sosa was a visiting player, fireworks lit up the sky—a joyous act that apparently made some Padre players furious. Indeed, the partisan San Diego crowd would not be stilled until Sosa had emerged from the dugout to take a curtain call—in the visiting ballpark!

The Cubs won the game 6–3 and Sosa had delivered in

the biggest way possible at the most electrifying moment possible—when the cameras were on and everyone was watching.

Our national game had been rescued from the abyss by Sosa and his friend McGwire. Americans took a few baby steps forward by embracing a Dominican whose English isn't perfect. And a movement in baseball—the accepted dominance of Latin players—became a huge story. With Sosa leading the way, Latin athletes now make up 25 percent of player rosters—a figure that looks to increase in the coming years.

As Sosa will reveal in the pages that follow, the road he took to where he is now sets him apart from every major athlete we know today.

There have been hints, glimpses of the world from which Sosa came. But never anything like this. When one considers how famous and successful he is and where he came from, it goes a long way toward explaining his lasting appeal.

Sosa is one of a kind. His is a great story, and the best thing of all is that it really happened.

And, as Sosa would say himself, the ride is far from over.

—Marcos Bretón
February 1, 2000

1

The Journey

People always ask me how I stay in shape over the winter when I'm home in my country, the Dominican Republic. Do I have a private gym? Do I have personal trainers? Do I practice on a custom-built, state-of-the-art baseball diamond? You certainly could afford all those things, people say to me. But let me tell you my secret. Three days a week during the off-season, I leave my house in the early afternoon to embark on a journey to a special place—the one place where I prepare for the season ahead. On this journey, I take my bats, my Chicago Cubs gear, and everything else I need to practice the craft of hitting, the skill that has brought me so many blessings and made me known to so many wonderful people.

As a way of saying thank you to all of you who have cheered me and filled my life with so much joy, I write this book and invite you on this journey. It is my hope that when we complete it together, there will be no doubting who I am and what I'm about.

I make this four-hour round trip (I'll tell you where we are going in a minute) to remind myself of where I came from, of what gives me strength, of what made me who I am. And every time I make it, the journey becomes a kind of celebration—not of home runs or millions of dollars, but of faith.

In fact, my life is a celebration of faith—faith in my abilities as a baseball player when no team wanted me, of my faith in God when my family and I were hungry and penniless. And faith in the most important, most cherished person in my life: my blessed mother, Mireya.

It is her I salute, with a touch to my heart and a kiss blown directly into the television cameras, every time I hit a home run. That simple gesture has become like a trademark for me, something that gets written about a lot in the newspapers and the magazines. In all those articles and on television, I always say, "I love you, Mama."

That love has sustained me all my life, all the way back to the place I return to again and again—first as a barefoot boy, now as a person of privilege. It is a town very familiar to baseball fans: San Pedro de Macorís, a city of hope and 200,000 residents.

Before anyone had ever heard of me, San Pedro was known as an amazing city that produced big-league players like no other. Tony Fernandez, who won multiple gold gloves with the Toronto Blue Jays, is from San Pedro. So is Pedro Guerrero, who starred with the Los Angeles Dodgers in the 1980s. Also from San Pedro are former American League MVP George Bell, and Rico Carty, who was the National League batting champion with the Atlanta Braves in 1970.

And so was pitcher Joaquin Andujar, who had back-to-back 20-win seasons with the St. Louis Cardinals in the 1980s. I could go on and on—they could probably assemble an all-star team made up only of San Pedro natives.

The other thing San Pedro is known for is sugarcane. Vendors sell it on street corners there, cutting small wedges and placing them snugly into plastic bags that people buy by the thousands.

There is nothing like it in the world. But garnering that sweet taste and developing a sweet swing in baseball come at a price of back-breaking work and sacrifice. I've paid that price in my life. So going back to the place where I started is like going back to the well for nourishment.

Once there, I often visit my mother, in the home I bought for her—just as I promised I would when I reached the big leagues. But mostly I go back to San Pedro to train, to work out, and to take my cuts in batting practice. Why? Because I could never think of training any place else—though my American friends would probably be amazed to see where I prepare for Greg Maddux, Randy Johnson, and Kevin Brown.

It's a park where I played as a child, the place where my friend Hector Peguero first saw me uncork a throw from right field as I do now in the big leagues. My brother Luis had taken me to Hector, who was recognized in my town for knowing a lot about baseball. Hector took one look at me, saw my arm strength, turned to my brother and said, *"Hay comida."* Loosely translated to English, that means, "That arm could pay for a lot of food." But I'm getting ahead of myself. I'll come back to that story later.

As we approach the small playground in San Pedro, I'm transported back in time. Whenever my vehicle pulls up, it provides quite a contrast to the humble surroundings. Bumping along a dirt road that leads to a ragged baseball diamond with no infield grass, I witness the same scene each time I come here. Running along each side of my vehicle are young children dressed in stained T-shirts and cut-off shorts. Some shout out my name: "Sammy! Sammy!"

Turning onto the field, I pull up to the third-base dugout. The field itself is rough compared to the baseball diamonds in America. There are stones all over the infield. The outfield grass is hard and patchy. The dugouts are made of stone and painted green—though the paint has been chipping since I was a kid.

The backstop is a sagging, chain-link fence, and there are no bleachers to speak of. The park is in a modest, working-class neighborhood and is filled with small, barefoot children, just like I used to be.

There is great poverty in my country, and it surrounds this park. I used to shine shoes near here. I used to live near here, in a one-bedroom house with dirt floors and no indoor plumbing. Those kinds of dwellings have not disappeared with the passage of time. The people who are always waiting for me at the park in San Pedro live that way today. These are my people.

They know my routine, they look forward to seeing me. And I look forward to seeing them. As I step out of my vehicle, the people are joyous but respectful, coming close to touch but not crowding in as a mob.

Once in the dugout, I have to crouch down to avoid bumping my head on the ceiling. Then I change into my familiar gear: dark blue Cubs shirt, white pants with blue stripes, dark blue baseball spikes.

I tape my wrists, as I do before every game in Wrigley and every other park in the National League. Once ready, my old friend Hector joins me. He still lives here in San Pedro, helping young people learn baseball properly. Other people who have known me since I was a boy are here, too. But they don't call me Sammy. They call me Mikey. That's a nickname that was given to me by my grandmother, who heard the name on a soap opera she liked and decided that from that moment on I would be Mikey. To this day, my mother calls me Mikey. My brothers and sisters call me Mikey. All my old friends call me Mikey. And everyone who comes to the park in San Pedro to watch me practice calls me Mikey, too.

It's a nickname that's so familiar and so closely linked to me that it's become very personal. Everything about my visits to San Pedro is personal and special.

Once I'm dressed, I love to jog around the rough diamond at San Pedro, as I would for any practice on the classic, manicured diamond at Wrigley. I always go once around, all the way around the infield and then the outfield—right, center, and left—and back up the third-base line. By the time I finish my trot, a big crowd has assembled. The people stand behind a long rope down the third-base line, or they stand behind the rusted chain-link fence that acts as a backstop.

I then do calisthenics with my friends in the same way I would do them with teammates on the Cubs. Then we'll do wind sprints in the outfield. Sometimes I do them with a number of small children running along with me. People always ask me how I was able to keep my concentration during the great home run race of 1998, when my friend Mark McGwire and I closed in on Roger Maris's record with the media following us like an army. What I said then is what I would say if people asked how I train seriously with so many people around: I have the kind of concentration where I can shut everything off and focus on what I need to do.

Here in San Pedro, I work out hard no matter how many kids show up, no matter how many adults compete for my attention, tell me their problems, ask for help, or try to get me interested in some idea or some detail they just have to share with me. This is who I am—I love being around people.

Soon it's time for batting practice. Pulling out my own personalized bats, I start slowly and build momentum, lashing home runs and line drives that would go out of any major league park. By the time I get to batting practice, the golden sun of my beautiful island is at its most spectacular. One of the things I love so much about my island nation is the weather. With few exceptions, it's almost always 85 degrees. I think if Mr. Cub, Ernie Banks, lived in the Dominican, he'd say, "Let's play two—maybe three—every day."

On this day, a few months before the start of the 2000 season, the balls are flying out, leaping off my bat. I feel strong at the start of a new year. And I'm looking forward to this year like no other because I feel like I'm at the top of my game.

After taking my hacks, I love to sit on a chair very near home plate and watch the local kids, eagerly dressed in baseball uniforms that dangle off their skinny frames, as they take batting practice. I smile as young pitchers and catchers throw that little bit extra into what they are doing, showing off for me. I offer words of encouragement to these kids because for a lot of my youth, encouragement was in very short supply.

My mother always taught me that it doesn't cost anything to be kind to people, to be generous with your heart. And really, by spending time this way, I get as much as I give. After each workout, I feel good and love to stop and talk with people. One by one they approach me, men and women bringing their children, all standing close to me for a picture. There are old friends, too, who knew me when I was young and who talk about old times and laugh with me. Yes, I posed for a lot of pictures this past winter.

Those moments fill me with satisfaction because I still view myself as I always have—as a human being, no better or no worse than anyone else. It's because of these feelings and these beliefs that I think people have been drawn to me.

But what I am today I am because of mother. I treat people well because that's what she taught me. I work hard and do my best because I saw her give her all every day of her life, and she didn't get paid millions of dollars to do it. And I'm grateful for all that I have because in this life everything ends except God—so you should be humble and grateful. I am.

It's been said that athletes have grown distant from the fans because of all the money they make. In my own small way, I'd like to think I'm proving that it doesn't always have to be that way.

Soon, it's time to go home. By the time we get back on the road, I'm dripping sweat, though my workouts don't end there. Like a lot of ballplayers, I'm a night owl—I stay up late and get up late. And a lot of times, as late as 1:00 or 2:00 A.M., I'll work out in my home gym, getting my body prepared for the rigors of a 162-game season.

As the season approached in 2000, my workouts became more grueling, my concentration more focused. I'm not going to predict 60 home runs or anything of that kind for this season, but I do expect a lot of myself right now—at thirty-one, I'm in my prime. As I'm driven back to Santo Domingo, I spend much of my time dealing with the hectic schedule brought on by many commitments.

Chief among them is my commitment to my country, a responsibility I take very seriously. I've made commercials praising the Dominican Republic for its beauty as a tourist destination. I established a foundation that benefits needy Dominican families—a twenty-four-hour job, because there is much need in my country. I have another foundation in my adopted country, the United States. It's the least I could do because America has been so good to me through the years. I mean, how many people get to meet the president of the United States, get to light the national Christmas tree at the White House, and then get singled out at a State of the Union address? It's amazing to me to think about it, but I've gotten to do all those things. So make no mistake, I love America.

The light of my life is my wife and my four children, who depend on me to be husband and father. When I get home, they are all waiting for me, along with my five brothers and sisters, who come and go through my house as if it were their own. That's the way we were always taught by my mother, to love one another and share with one another. That I can help them all today to live better lives is one of the joys in my life. All that love is waiting for me as I turn down the avenue that leads back to my home.

There was once a time when I couldn't even afford to buy myself a bus ticket from San Pedro to Santo Domingo, and now I ride back and forth between the two homes—the two extremes in my life—as if I were a king. It's been a long journey to get to where I am today. I always thought I would get here, I just didn't know how. The journey isn't over, of course. There is still a long way to go. But sometimes I can't believe where I am now, so far from San Pedro, from the place where I started, at a time when everyone knew me as Mikey.

2

Mikey

By now everybody knows I was a shoe-shine boy. As a boy, I would always rise early in the morning to shine shoes so at the end of the day I could give the money to my mother.

My father died when I was six. I recall very little about him, but what I do remember about my father was that he was the best there was. His name was Juan Bautista Montero. As is the custom in some parts of my country, my siblings and I took my mother's maiden name, Sosa, after my father's death. She was all we had left.

When I was a small child, I would get up in the mornings, and my dad would be sitting at the table eating breakfast. I used to love to sit next to him and just watch him. And he would catch me looking at him and sometimes sit me in his lap and feed me a little from his plate.

And when it was time for him to leave, he would always slip me a little money so I could go out and buy myself something. When my father was alive, there were opportunities for advancement for our family.

My father drove a tractor. His job was to clear brush in open fields and prepare the land for planting sugarcane. My dad wasn't a big man, but he was strong, and he had a very strong work ethic.

My father was very affectionate with us. And he was also a very honest person, someone who was very stoic, very calm, and very conservative with money. Everyone in town knew him and respected him.

He loved baseball and was a fan of the local team, Licey, one of the best teams in the Dominican Winter League. But he didn't have time to play much himself; he was always too busy working. None of my other relatives were athletes either, so people always ask me how I got my natural ability. I always say I was blessed with it but that my parents gave me something much more important than the ability to hit a baseball: they gave me love and a work ethic.

My mother was working for a living by the time she was a young girl. Her given name is Lucrecia, but everyone calls her Mireya. Like my father, she came from a humble family and had to quit school at an early age. My mother worked as a maid, cleaning the homes of wealthy people. And she got married at a young age, though not to my father. That marriage didn't last. She was divorced after the birth of her first child, my eldest brother, Luis. After her divorce she was a single, working mother, long before anyone ever used that phrase. She found work in a town called Consuelo and was living alone when she met my father.

My mother says she fell in love with him right away because he was a serious man as well as a gentleman. They got married in 1963, right there in Consuelo, which is about 50 miles east of Santo Domingo. It's a small town, a farming town. Most people work the sugarcane fields nearby and live in houses rented to them by the sugar companies.

That's how my family lived. We used to have to take our water from an outside source because the water running through the taps was not drinkable.

I came along on November 12, 1968—a big, healthy baby, Mama says. They named me Samuel because it was a biblical name that my maternal grandmother—the same one who nicknamed me Mikey—liked very much. Today, all my records say that I was born in San Pedro de Macorís, the largest town nearby. I love San Pedro. It's where I became what I am today, and I have such fond memories of it that in my new house I had artists create a series of stained-glass windows with street scenes of the downtown area.

But in truth I was born in Consuelo. I didn't actually live in San Pedro until I was almost thirteen years old. In Consuelo, when I was very young, all I did was go to school and play with my friends. What memories I have of those early days are happy ones. My dad had his job and my mom, because she was such a good cook, prepared food and sold it to people. We were doing okay.

But that all changed in the summer of 1975. My father had been sick and feeling weak. One day, while he was on his tractor, he had terrible headaches. He was taken to the doctor there in Consuelo. He gave him medicine, and my mother says he felt a little better. But the doctor gave us a warning: "Take your husband to a hospital in Santo Domingo, where they can give him proper tests. He's very sick."

My mother begged my father to go, but he kept insisting he was all right. I don't know if he knew how sick he was, but he kept telling my mother, "I have to work." And off he would go. There were always jobs for him. And all my dad had to do was to look at all the children in his house for an incentive to keep pushing.

But my mother was so worried. She knew something was wrong. About a month later something happened that still brings her to tears. And when she tells the story, her normally

sunny voice drops to a whisper. Whenever she talks this way,
I know what she's remembering.

Mireya Sosa:

It was early morning, and my husband was going to work.
He was such a kind, decent man, so hard-working. We always
got along so well because he was very kind to the children and
me. We understood each other very well.

That morning he said, *"Mi amor* (my love), why don't you
prepare dinner early today? I'll work a half day and come
home early so we can eat with the children."

I responded: *"Sí, mi amor."* (Yes, my love.)

So he went off to work, and I cleaned around the house until it was time to go to the market. I was going to prepare a big
dinner that night. I was at the market, buying food, when suddenly I saw one of my sons come running up to me. I knew
immediately what was wrong.

"Mommy, Mommy!" he cried. "There's something wrong
with Dad!" I dropped the food and started running. I went to
a clinic there in Consuelo, but he wasn't there. I went to another one, but he wasn't there either. I was frantic. I couldn't
find him.

What I didn't know was that some people in town had
taken him to San Pedro, a short distance away. He had been
on his tractor when he had another attack. This one was much
worse—it was a cerebral hemorrhage.

We took him to Santo Domingo, where he was admitted to
a clinic. At first we had hope, but his condition got much
worse. The doctor called us and gave us the news: my beloved
husband was going to die.

So we decided as a family to take him home, to go back to

Consuelo so he could at least die in his own house. He lay in bed for a time, and I gathered my children close to him. His family all came, too. And we waited with him.

When the time came and he left us to go to God, the family was all together. Sammy doesn't have any memories of that day, but my older children do. It was August 30, 1975.

When I lost Sammy's father, I suffered so much, and I felt so alone, so sad. And what hurt me the most in those terrible first days was when I would look into the faces of my children and know that they would now be raised without their father. That is very difficult. And then I realized that now it was me who was going to have to provide for these children.

Luis was fourteen. Sammy was six. Jose Antonio, my youngest, was four. And I had another boy and two girls in between. My parents have always helped me, but they were really short on money themselves, so they couldn't help very much at all. And it's sad to say, but my husband's family forgot about us after my husband died. We were all alone.

Sammy:

What I remember most about those days was working—we all worked. I started going out with my brothers, shining shoes. We would also take a bucket of water and some soap and wash whatever cars we could.

My mother cooked for people, she sold lottery tickets, and she worked day and night. Because of what had happened, the only thing we could do was to unite as a family. My mother always told us we had to stick together, so all us kids became very close. We would share everything. We shared our food, we shared our clothing. If one of us didn't have any shoes to wear, we would borrow from each other. My brother

Luis became my hero. I saw how hard he worked for us, and he always watched out for me; he let me go with him wherever he went.

For the next three years we stayed in Consuelo, but things were very hard. I was getting up early in the morning to shine shoes. Then I would go to school until the late afternoon. Then I would work with my brothers washing cars until really late at night. Whenever I could, I would play baseball in the park, but the truth is I didn't have much time for the game. The other thing I did a lot was fight. I was always fighting with the neighborhood kids. I loved to fight and would never back down from any challenge. I wasn't afraid of anyone.

But things were getting worse and worse at home. There just weren't any opportunities in Consuelo. When my father was alive, we always ate three solid meals a day. There was always food in the house. But now, even with my mother working nonstop and us helping her, we started to go hungry. Sometimes we only had two meals a day, sometimes only one. We ate a lot of rice and beans, fried plantains and Yucca.

But if my mother was ever scared or worried, she never showed it. We all depended on her, and she never wavered. People ask me now why I blow a kiss to my mother after all my home runs. I always say there are many reasons for that, and they go all the way back to our days in Consuelo.

I remember one conversation in particular. My mother came up to me—I was probably eight or nine—and said, "*Mijo* (my son), your mother doesn't have money for food tomorrow. Do you think you could go out and work and bring some money home?"

I said, "Sí, Mommy. Don't worry. I'll bring home some money." That day I went out and worked really, really hard shining shoes. And I brought back money for my mother, money she used to buy food. I would do anything for her because I knew she would do anything for me.

Above all, she instilled in us a deep sense of honesty. She always said that whatever money or things we brought into our house had to come from the sweat of our brows. Where we lived there were lots of kids who were poor like us but who carried a lot of money sometimes. Or you would see them with a nice piece of clothing. They would tell their parents that they had found it or something—or that someone had given them a gift.

Most times their parents would look the other way, say they believed them when they really didn't. But my mother would have never permitted that. If we had ever brought something home that she knew we hadn't earned, she would have gone with us to take it back.

Despite her honesty, things just kept getting worse and worse financially. My brothers and I would be staying out really late at night, working. Sometimes we wouldn't get home until midnight or one in the morning.

What we would do is go to the nice part of town, see a car parked in the street, and wash it. Then we'd have to sit there and wait until the owner came out so we could ask him if he would give us any money for washing his car. Sometimes that would take hours. My brothers and I would have to stand there, waiting and waiting.

We'd laugh and joke with each other, but those hours spent waiting, trapped in a way because we couldn't afford to leave, made a big impression on me. When you don't have any control over your economic situation, when your stomach is empty, when you see your mother working so hard and you have to stand around for hours, waiting for someone, it leaves a mark on you.

That experience made me realize how hard it is to earn money, and it burned inside me that I didn't want to live this way for the rest of my life. Sometimes we wouldn't even get paid—all those hours wasted!

But, as in so many other facets of my life, those moments taught me once again how much my mother loved us. As tired as she was from working, she just couldn't lay herself down to sleep for the night unless all her children were home. So we'd be out, waiting to collect money for washing cars, and she'd be home, looking out the window for us. Sometimes she couldn't bear to wait, and she would come out looking for us.

Looking back then, we boys didn't understand completely why our mother would be out at 1:00 A.M. hunting us down. In fact, I remember we'd get embarrassed if our friends made fun of us. She'd find us and we'd explain to her, "Mommy, we can't leave. We washed these cars and we have to wait until the people come out so we can collect some money." Sometimes we'd all go home together. We were poor and we weren't building much of a bank account, but as a family we were building something a lot more important.

By 1978, when I was nine, my mother decided that we could no longer stay in Consuelo. She felt like we had to go to a place where there were more people and more opportunities to make money. So we moved to the big city—the capital, Santo Domingo. But because we were so poor, we could only afford to live in a barrio, with other poor people. Life in Santo Domingo was much different from life in Consuelo. Consuelo is very tranquil, very peaceful. But Santo Domingo, especially in the barrios, is scary. There were always drugs around, and a lot of the young people were involved in gangs. There was corruption everywhere.

Looking back now, I think my mother feels like she made a mistake by moving us to Santo Domingo, but we were desperate for money. And by cooking and preparing food, my mother was making more than she had in Consuelo. I was going to school less and less and working more and more. I remember all of us feeling very alone back then.

To this day the people closest to me are my family because there weren't many people around who I could trust. By this point my brother Luis was regularly defending me, keeping some of the bigger boys in our barrio from doing anything to me or my younger brother, Jose Antonio.

We lived in really crowded conditions. We all slept in the same room. Our roof was made of corrugated metal, and I remember all the houses were pressed hard against each other. There was always garbage in the streets and raw sewage. It was not uncommon to see little babies naked in the streets because people where we lived couldn't afford diapers sometimes.

In the United States, some people survive on welfare so they can eat. But it's hard here because you don't have anyone who can help you. You don't have a life; you don't have a chance. I know what it is to be hungry. We had some critical moments during these years. There were days when we had no food.

Everyone knows that when you eat, you feel good. But if you don't eat, what you feel is sadness—a strong anxiety. The only thing I could do at this point in my life was to keep pushing forward.

My brothers and I were very serious about making money, any honest way we could. And I was really lucky—though I had few friends, I had good examples to follow. Along with my mother, I had my brother Luis.

I remember that Luis worked really hard and would give his money to Mama. But I found out that he was holding back a little for himself. He was keeping it in a little container that kept getting more and more full.

But then I remember that once the container was full, he gave that to my mother. It was like an added surprise for her, something that she wasn't expecting. That's what poor people do—you look for little ways to find hope.

And, luckily for us, my mother always gave us hope. By this point she was washing clothes, too. It was during this time that my mother taught us to keep God in our hearts. She would take us to church, and we would pray as a family. She was doing everything she could do to keep us on the right path, but after nine months in Santo Domingo, it became clear that we had to leave.

There were just too many bad influences for us kids; there was too much crime and too much danger. So, we moved back to the country, to a place called Caciques. My mother had remarried, to a decent man named Carlos Maria Peralta. But our financial situation was still critical. For the next two years we moved around a couple of times. It seemed like we were always moving. I didn't have much of a chance to focus on my schoolwork because of our situation.

As I said, we felt very alone back then and kept feeling that way until my mother made the best decision we ever could have made—we were moving to San Pedro de Macorís.

It was a good-sized city where we had family and people we knew; it wasn't wild like Santo Domingo or desperate like the country. We would try to make a new start and find a way to keep surviving. San Pedro had lots of nice parks and places to play. What my mother loved best was that, unlike Santo Domingo, she knew where to find us in San Pedro if she ever went looking for us. There were only so many places to go.

We moved to San Pedro in 1981, when I was twelve. I was pretty tough by this point and, in my own way, quiet and reserved. Maybe I took after my father because my mom likes to say that she saw a lot of him in me. Like him, I liked to keep my private things private. I was careful with the little money I had; I kept my plans to myself and shared them only after I decided what I was going to do.

I liked San Pedro right away, and it became clear to my

brothers and me that we could make money here. We staked out a place in the main square of town where we would shine the shoes of businessmen who worked in the sugar industry or in the factories in the nearby Zona Franca, an industrial park.

San Pedro is a working town filled with working people and factories. Later, I took a job in one of those factories—a job that changed my life. But at first, our primary source of income was shining the shoes of the better-off working people of San Pedro. My brothers and I developed a steady stream of customers.

We learned that if we were going to make any money over the long term, we were going to have to develop a list of clients who would become loyal to us and seek us out when they needed shines. There was a lot of competition in San Pedro because there were plenty of poor kids like us and only so many people who needed their shoes shined.

We would literally fight with the other kids to keep our customers to ourselves. My brother Luis was very smart, too. With some of his money, he bought some more shoe-shining boxes and soon had talked some younger kids into working for him.

They would shine shoes and give him half of what they earned. And what we found was that if we treated our customers well, they would come back again and again. There were some kids who would try and cheat their customers, charging them too much for a shine. But Luis always said that we shouldn't do that. After a while, people would catch on and they would get their shines from somebody else. For us, there was no way we could let that happen. We kept going on this way until one day, I met one of the most important people in my life.

His name is William Chase, but we always called him Bill. He is an American, from Bristol, Maine, and to us, back then, he was the richest man we had ever met. He owned a shoe factory in San Pedro in those days and employed a lot of people in our town. He was important, and we knew it. We started out by shining his shoes. He got to like us, and we got to like him even though we couldn't really communicate because we didn't speak English and he didn't speak Spanish. But we hit it off. He liked the way we shined his shoes, and he would smile at how hard we worked to keep the other kids away from him. He kept coming back to us again and again.

And before too long, he was impressed enough to make us an offer. He gave my brothers and me jobs in his factory. Our task would be to sweep the whole place, a tough job because it was very big. Soon I was sweeping big pieces of leather off the factory floors. I was cleaning the machinery that assembled soles, insteps, and heels and laced the shoes together. It was tough work, but I was happy because the work was stable.

I worked from 8:00 A.M. until about 4:00 P.M., and often I worked a lot later. I made 300 pesos a week—about $20 in today's money but more back then when the exchange rate was different. Believe me, that was a lot of money in those days. I was very happy in my job, but I was facing a decision in another part of my life that had to be made.

I sat down and talked to my mother and explained to her that continuing in school was becoming more and more difficult. In my country most people like us don't get the chance to go to college. There is just too much pressure to work and earn a living. I enjoyed studying. It came easily to me. But in the equivalent of the eighth grade, I left. Still, I was happy because by working full-time I was helping my mother. We were still very poor, but things weren't critical the way they had been earlier in my life. And I was growing closer and closer to Bill. When we needed to communicate directly, we would do so through an interpreter, another man who worked at the factory.

As our relationship grew, Bill and his wife began to treat us as if we were their children. When they would go back to the United States for visits, they would bring us toys and candy. We would tell our mother how nice Bill was, too; she would smile and tell us that God always rewarded people who did hard work. And to me Bill was like our reward.

Bill Chase:

I had opened a shoe factory in San Pedro de Macorís. I had a gentleman from San Pedro who was helping me get started. He was bilingual. I remember that after the first day of work, he took me to a place where we could eat in the downtown area, in the square. San Pedro has a square like all the towns in the Dominican Republic, and everybody hangs out there, including all the kids washing cars, shining shoes, running errands, making a few cents.

As we got there, there were probably two or three hundred kids. Now there probably weren't that many, but it seemed like it; there were kids all over the square. And all of a sudden, two of these kids come up. And Juan, the man who was working with me, introduced them to me. One of them was Sammy, but he was introduced to me as Mikey. And he had his younger brother, Jose, with him. Juan said to me, "These are two good boys, they will shine your shoes for you." And right away I took a liking to them because they were aggressive, they knew how to handle a customer. They knew how to get a dollar off of the streets. If I didn't like something that was just right on the shoes or something, they would work at it until they got it the way I liked it. Anyway, things progressed between me and them, and they kept shining my shoes.

In those days there was a college in San Pedro that had about five thousand American students. It was a medical college, and nearby there was a place to eat called Restaurant 29. An English lady ran the place, and all the Americans went there to eat. After a week of going down to the square to eat and having Sammy and his brother shine my shoes, I quit going and started eating with all the other Americans. But Sammy found me. Eventually they would be sitting outside the restaurant waiting for me and, after a while, I would always save some chicken for them or whatever.

Back then, the industrial part of San Pedro—the Free Zone, as they called it—was very small. There were only six factories. Later, there were ninety. But back then, there was just a handful of Americans with money. Not that I had money, but to Sammy I did. So there was always a fight among the kids over the gringo. I remember the first day we got a load of machinery in for the shoe factory, I hired this guy who we knew as Pepe. His real name was Luis Carasso. He could get you what you wanted. I hired him to get a bunch of people to unload my trailer, and he became like my bodyguard.

Pepe and the boys were always jealous of each other because in their minds they were scrambling for the same peso. It wasn't really that way, but in their minds it was. I always used to tell the boys, "*No trabajo, no dinero*"—no work, no money.

So they could make money, I would always find something for Sammy and his brother to do. And I always made sure I got them food from the restaurant. I would give them chicken, and Sammy and his brother would always eat it and pick the meat off the bones.

Pretty soon Sammy and his brother were shining my shoes every day. And I'd give them each a peso. They and Pepe were like my center there in San Pedro. Whenever I gave

Pepe a peso, he would go buy his beer, but the boys always took theirs home to Mama. Because of the competition between them, pretty soon the boys started coming over to the factory. It was as though they didn't want to lose their place in life. This was before I got to know them as part of the family. They were just kids doing stuff for me.

At this point my wife was back in the States working, and I kept telling her about them. Finally she came down, and one day she wanted some apples. I told her that the apples in the Dominican weren't the same as the ones in the States, that they were real mushy and that she wouldn't like them. But she had Sammy's brother Jose go to the store and buy her four apples. Well, she took a bite and didn't like it. So she said to the boys, "Just throw them away."

So they both look at her and say, "Is it okay if we take these home to our mother?" Well, that was it. She fell in love with them right there.

From then on, whenever she came to visit, she always brought them clothes or whatever they wanted, but basically clothes. In those days, all those boys knew about was the necessities. They didn't know anything about the good side of life. So as my business started developing, I started hiring some of their brothers and sisters to work in the factory.

Sammy:

We grew to depend on Bill. When things were tough at home, we would ask Bill for a little more money, and he would help us. What he expected was for us to work hard for him, and we did. I can say today that I began to look upon Bill as a father figure. When I was twelve years old, he bought me my very first bike, and I can never remember being so happy. I loved that bike and rode it everywhere.

Things were coming together for us then, and it was like a cloud was being lifted. I remember two things most of all from my childhood. The first was a Mother's Day when I was very young and things were still critical for us. I didn't have a dime to my name, and I felt really bad that I didn't have any-thing to give my mother. It was starting to get late in the day, and I felt like I had to do something. So I did—something that my friends and fans probably wouldn't believe today. On this day, to help ease my mother's burden and bring a smile to her face, I went out into the street and begged for money. I needed to get money somehow so I could buy her something, and I wasn't going to go home until I did. Luckily, some peo-ple took pity on me and gave me a few cents. I then went to a store, where I asked the shopkeeper if I could buy a gift for my mother—a single cigarette. My mother enjoyed smoking then, so I wanted to buy her something she could enjoy. I was nine years old.

With the cigarette in my hand, I went back home and found my mother, sitting and talking with some of her girl-friends. I walked up to her and said, "Mommy, I don't have much to give you, but I give you this with all my heart on Mother's Day."

She took me in her arms and said, "What a beautiful present you've given me, son. Thank you, thank you."

I've given her so much since then, but that might have been the most meaningful thing I ever did for her—it came straight from my heart. We had been through so much to-gether up to that point that I wanted to do something for her. My mother still remembers that day vividly, and so do I. It was an example of the love she had created for us in our home. And I think it shows that when you love someone, you'll do anything for him or her.

As I said, by the time we had moved to San Pedro things had gotten a little easier, and life was starting to take me in a different direction. I was overjoyed with the bike that Bill had given me, but after one of his trips back to the United States, he had another present for me. Like the bike, it was something I always wanted but could never afford. This gift would point me in a direction that I couldn't see then but appears so clearly today.

On that day Bill gave me my first baseball glove.

Bill Chase:

When Sammy was about thirteen, I got him the glove. It was a blue glove, and I paid about a hundred dollars for it. It was an excellent glove, the best you could find. The key is, it was blue. You might notice that today Sammy only wears blue gloves.

Anyway, around this time I was just opening my second factory, and I didn't have a lot of time for anything. But pretty soon, everybody was raving about what a good ballplayer he was. And I'm asking myself, "How good can he be since he only started playing ball at thirteen or fourteen?" But he was a natural, as we all discovered later.

Jose Antonio was doing all my customers' shoes, and Sammy was out doing the baseball thing. Sammy would come by the factory once in a while just to keep me posted on things or to pick up five or ten pesos.

At that time one of my plant managers had married a local girl, and her family had seen Sammy play and said he was really good. So one day I said to my manager, "Listen, let's take a couple of hours and go watch Sammy play." So we did. It was nothing spectacular, but he was very agile and fast. He

had the only good glove in town, and he was making plays
that maybe if he didn't have the glove he wouldn't have made.
He was looking pretty good. I remember thinking, "Someday,
if he keeps growing, with a little bit of experience, this kid
could make the big time."

3

My First Contract

In my country small boys begin playing baseball not long after they learn to walk. In every town and village in any part of the island, you'll see them playing pick-up games in the streets, in alleys, in parks, and open fields. When I was a boy, baseball was the only sport in the Dominican. It's still our national game. The people here follow it the year round. From April to October, Dominicans are glued to their television sets and scan the box scores of the major-league baseball season, just as Americans do.

And from November to February, the whole island closely follows the Dominican Winter League, whose teams are filled mostly with Dominican major leaguers who use the winter to hone their skills.

Also in February is the Caribbean World Series, a tournament where our league champion competes against the league champions from Puerto Rico, Venezuela, and Mexico. Each country takes turns hosting the tournament, and it's always a huge source of pride when we win—which we have done many times. During those games Dominican flags are everywhere, and my people show their national pride and deep love for the game of baseball. Along with Dominican Independence Day, which is February 27, Caribbean Series time is always a special series of days for my country.

There is a passion for baseball in my country that I love. People here build life-long allegiances to local teams— Estrellas Orientales, Licey, Escogido, Aguilas, and so on— just as Americans do for the Yankees, Mets, Dodgers or Cubs. And for young people there are dozens of little-league and amateur leagues in every region of the Dominican Republic.

Boys practice for those leagues all week long and play intense games on the weekends. It's no wonder there are so many Dominican players in the big leagues today because, for our young boys, baseball is everything. Everybody here knows that big-league teams have scouts all over the island, just as they know there is an even bigger network of people who follow even the most remote amateur-league games in the hope of seeing a flash of talent that they can then recommend to a scout.

But despite this history, which goes back many years, I didn't play any organized baseball as a young boy. I didn't have the love for the game back then, which made me the exception to the rule. Our financial situation was so critical I simply didn't have the time to do much else besides work and earn money. When I did play baseball, I played on the street, using balled-up rags for baseballs and sticks for bats. That's a lot different from working with coaches and drilling in fundamentals. In my life, in my preteen years, coaches and ball games complete with uniforms was something for other kids.

I didn't have any plans to play organized baseball. Though Bill Chase had been nice enough to give me my first real baseball glove, I wanted to be an athlete of another kind—a professional fighter.

I wanted to be like Sugar Ray Leonard, Tommy Hearns, and Marvin Hagler. In the early 1980s, those fighters were the kings of boxing, and I loved the way they fought. I had fought a lot in the streets when I was a kid, defending myself and proving to the other kids that I was tough. So already having the inclination, I found out San Pedro had a boxing school soon after we moved there. Soon I was attending, squeezing training sessions in between my work hours at Bill Chase's shoe factory.

I used to get up early in the morning and do road work. I would spar, and hit the speed bag and the heavy bag. I trained hard for months. There haven't been many well-known fighters from the Dominican, but that didn't worry me. The truth is, I wanted to be a champion boxer.

In our family it was my brother Luis who loved baseball, who played the game and knew the game. It was his passion, and he tried to get me interested, but I had my own plans. And as I had done since I was a small child, I kept them to myself. Luis knew what I was doing, but I hadn't discussed my goal of a boxing career with my mother. Maybe I knew in my heart that she wouldn't approve. So I told myself I would tell her later—much later.

It went on this way for almost a year. In a way, I was already living like an adult. I had quit school, was working long hours, and was spending my time on my goals. And I knew how to fight. I was good at it, even though my fans probably wouldn't have recognized me back then. Like a lot of Dominican kids of my background, I was very thin and hadn't come close to developing physically. All I had was a lot of desire.

I thought I had what it took to be a fighter, but, fortunately for me, the people who loved me the most had other ideas. My mother remembers it like it was yesterday.

Mireya Sosa:

One day Luis came up to me and said, "Mom, did you know that Sammy is practicing to be a boxer?"

I thought, "No. I don't want my son to be a fighter." I was terribly worried, but I knew, because Sammy was such a serious boy, that I had to find the right way to tell him. Luis said, "Mom, I don't want Sammy to think that I'm betraying a confidence."

And I reassured Luis that I would find the right way. For the next two weeks that's all I thought about, and I tried to find the words. Sammy had always been a good and obedient boy, but I still worried about saying the right thing. Then, one day, we were alone together, and I decided it was time. I said, "Son, come sit down here, I want to talk to you."

"Sí, Mama."

"Son, I've come to know that you are boxing, and I want to ask you to please stop. With all my heart I'm asking you to give it up. Please don't do it anymore."

"Why, Mom?"

"Son, hear me when I say this. Do you think that if you became a boxer that I could sit and watch you strike someone else or see someone hit you?"

"Mom, that would be no big deal."

"Son, it is a big deal. Do you know what it would be for a mother to see her own son getting hit? It would kill me to see that. No son, please don't do this. Please give this up." At that moment Sammy didn't say anything. I hoped he had listened to what I said because it hurt my heart to think of him exchanging punches with someone else.

Thank God, after some time passed, he gave me the wonderful news. "Mom," he announced, "I quit boxing."

"Oh, thank God, son. Thank God."

But he had another surprise for me. Sammy loves giving me surprises, as he did on Mother's Day when he was a boy.

That he wanted to tell me his plans made me feel at ease because I knew whatever it was would be better than his interest in boxing—which he had tried to keep from me. To my surprise, he told me he wanted to play baseball.

"You see, son! That's an idea I like! Baseball is a good thing for you to do because the only way you could get hurt is through bad luck, not because someone was trying to hurt you." I gave him my blessing, and from then on my son was a baseball player.

Sammy:

I could never do something like boxing if my mother was so opposed to it. I trusted her and valued her opinion, so I decided it wasn't for me. It was then that my brother Luis got me into baseball and set me on the path that I follow to this day.

I was able to get Bill Chase's permission to play ball a couple of days a week on work time. Once that happened, I started practicing baseball all the time, but it was still difficult for me because I had a lot of responsibility as well. At a certain point, I knew I needed to devote more time to baseball. So I talked to Bill Chase about it, and he agreed to hire my younger brother so our family wouldn't lose any income and I could continue to play ball.

When Bill Chase gave me his permission, my life became all about baseball. We were living in a two-room house near an abandoned hospital by this point, better than what we had known in Santo Domingo but still very humble. Like our other places, the house had dirt floors and one room that was cordoned off into sleeping quarters with bed sheets that my mother hung on ropes.

Every morning, I would get up at 6:00 A.M. and go to practice. I would run a lot and do anything I could to improve. I grew to love the game, but make no mistake: My dream was to help my mother.

It was while working at baseball that I realized I had talent. With my brother Luis, we would play in different barrios of San Pedro, with me learning something new with each game. Back then I always wore cut-off jeans, and I would practice on my street by hitting dried husks of maize again and again.

I would tell my friends that I was going to be a big-league ballplayer and they would say, "You're crazy. You're never going to amount to anything." But I never paid them any attention because I knew I had the dedication that set me apart from the others. By this point I had made up my mind what I was going to do with my life. I stayed out of trouble and remained very close to my mother and family. For me there weren't any days off. I worked at baseball every day.

And then, when he thought I was ready, Luis took me to see Hector Peguero, who had a reputation around San Pedro for knowing a lot about baseball. Hector ran a team in a local amateur league, and my brother knew he could help me.

Hector and I are still friends to this day, and I drive four hours, round-trip from my home in Santo Domingo, to practice with him and some other friends during the off-season. Sometimes, he still tells me when he sees something he doesn't like in my swing. And we still sometimes talk about that first day he saw me.

Hector Peguero:

Luis Sosa had played on a team that I ran, and so we knew each other. And one day, he initiated a conversation with me.

He said, "Hector, I have a kid with big hands who I want you to look at."

So he brought Sammy to the park, and the first thing I noticed was that he was strong. But he was also what we call here kind of a "lobo," which means kind of wild and raw. He didn't have much experience. I said, "Let's put him out on the field and see what he can do."

And so he started practicing with some other kids. He was playing in the outfield and then I saw him throw. Wow! He had a really strong arm.

Soon, I had gotten him onto my team in our league in San Pedro. We played with game uniforms, but his uniform didn't fit—he was a little bigger than the other kids on his team. So we moved him up to play against the bigger kids. And I swear, every time someone tried to run from second to home against him he would throw him out. One time the manager of another team accused Sammy of being a ringer. He claimed that Sammy was older than he really was. I said, "No, he's only fourteen."

Our team was in the Nelson Rodriguez League in San Pedro, playing in a park named after Rico Carty, the great hitter of the Atlanta Braves who is from San Pedro. It was there that Sammy Sosa hit his first home run. And his second home run was a grand slam!

At that time he was naturally hitting a lot to right field. He hardly ever pulled the ball to left. So I began working with him, showing him how to place his feet in the batter's box. He had this habit of pulling his leg to the left and hitting to right, and I tried to correct that.

He started to improve a lot because we were practicing Monday through Friday and playing games on Saturday and Sunday. So he began to develop. In our league he was sensational. In every game he would do something to surprise me. And he would always hit the ball hard.

Just like today, he gave everything he had, every time he played. What he still didn't know at that time was how to develop his talent, and that's what I was helping him with. I was working with 125 kids at that time, but Sammy began to stand out from the rest.

Sammy:

As I worked with Hector, my game began to improve, and I was starting to generate interest around San Pedro. The better I got, the more I wanted my loved ones to come see me play—especially my mother. After a year of playing with Hector, she still hadn't seen me play. I was fifteen by this point and was looking forward to showing her what I could do.

Mireya Sosa:

As time went by, my son Luis would say, "Mom, you should see Sammy play. You're going to make a lot of money off of him."

And I would say, in a scolding way, "Luis, he's only been playing a short time, and now you're telling me that I'm going to make a lot of money off of him!" Luis kept after me, but I never went because I was concerned for Sammy. I said, "Look, I'm not going to the park because if I go, and if he is playing well without me there, I know when he sees me, he is going to try even harder and maybe that will cause him to make a mistake."

And so I never went. One time, they played a game in San

Pedro that was televised. Oh my goodness! You should have seen the commotion! It was then that Sammy said, "Mom, come to the park and see me play."

I said, "No, son. I'm going to stay here at home and watch you on television." I was too nervous to go.

And so the whole house went to the game, and I stayed home alone and watched it. At first, I couldn't make out who Sammy was. A neighbor came over, pointed at the television, and said, "There's your son! There's your son!"

I said, "Where? Where?" I couldn't make him out from the other players until suddenly I recognized him. My goodness! What a feeling! There was my baby! He looked so beautiful!

When that game was over, Sammy had an even bigger surprise. He said, "Mom! Mom! They are going to sign me! They are going to sign me!" I didn't know what he was talking about—he was so excited. He then explained that a man named Acevedo who scouted for the Philadelphia Phillies was making him an offer to play professional baseball. Sammy said, "So Mom, you *have* to go to Santo Domingo tomorrow because they need you to sign the contract."

And I said, "Son, if it's for your benefit, you know I will be there."

So we went to Santo Domingo and met with Mr. Acevedo. I went along with my sons Luis and Sammy. He offered $2,500 as a signing bonus. The boys started talking about $3,000, and the discussion went around and around. Suddenly, I felt this feeling that I had never experienced, an overwhelming feeling that just took me over. I thought, "My God! I feel like I'm selling my own child!" It was just this huge feeling that came over me. I said to the boys, "No, no. Don't argue, don't argue. Let's be satisfied with what we have." And so that's what we accepted: $2,500. We signed the contract.

As we were leaving, Sammy said, "Mom! If you hadn't said anything we would have gotten more money!"

I just looked at him and said, "No, son. Don't think that way. Be satisfied with what God gives you, and you won't go wrong."

He understood what I meant, and we never discussed it again. Then Sammy started practicing very hard. And he started waiting for his money. And waiting and waiting and waiting.

Sammy:

At that time Mr. Acevedo had his own training camp, and he would sign players young and hide them until they were mature enough to be sent to the United States. Many of my American friends don't know what baseball recruiting is like in my country. Today, there are rules saying that a player has to be sixteen before he can be signed to a contract and that teams can only hold onto a player for a month. If, after that month, they don't sign him, the player is free to go to another team.

But back in 1984, when I was fifteen and was signed by the Phillies, those rules didn't exist. Scouts would hide and steal players from one another. As a player all you wanted was to be a professional, and you would go with whoever would help you do that. And you would sign for any amount of money. So when Acevedo approached me, I was very happy and emotional because I knew I had an opportunity to be a professional.

Top draft choices in the United States have agents and lawyers. But I didn't know anything back then. All I knew was baseball. The important thing was to play. Despite this I remember that signing the contract was the happiest moment in my life up to that point. The bonus check hadn't arrived yet, so Mr. Acevedo gave me a little bit of money out of his own pocket.

I hardly had any good clothes, so I went out and bought myself a nice pair of jeans and a pair of tennis shoes. I was so happy and so was my entire family. Everything was great. I even bought myself a little blue bicycle. But to tell the truth, I never knew what was on the paper that I signed with the Phillies. To this day I don't know. That was the way then. You were totally innocent and unprepared for negotiations—not a good way to be in the harsh business world of baseball, as I would discover over time. It wasn't long before I came to understand that something was wrong.

I would practice and practice with Mr. Acevedo, but my bonus money never came. In those years he was known on the island as an important scout. People who worked for him had discovered George Bell and Julio Franco. Today, everyone knows that Bell was AL MVP in 1987 for the Toronto Blue Jays and that Franco won a batting title for the Texas Rangers. I would see those men on the street in San Pedro during the off-season, and I would want to be like them. I saw how they dressed and marveled at the respect they commanded. I wanted that, too. And I wasn't alone.

There were thirty or forty other players Mr. Acevedo had under contract with the same ambition as me. But months and months went by and still no money.

To the people in our barrio, I was a professional ballplayer. But my family knew the truth, they knew how bad I was starting to feel about my first contract.

Mireya Sosa:

He was desperate. I had never seen him that way before. He would say, "Mom, this man still hasn't paid me yet."

I would say, "It's okay, son. He's going to pay you. You'll

see." We talked about it a lot. He tried to keep his anguish to himself, but I know my children. And I knew how much this was bothering him.

Sammy:

I kept working hard. And I did a lot of praying. I would tell my mother not to worry, that I would get the money for her. And she would tell me not to worry. The whole time I was with Mr. Acevedo, I never knew when I was going to get paid. He would give me a little bit of money here and there. But he never gave me the full $2,500—the money that I really needed.

A lot of time went by, about nine months of waiting. I would keep going to his office and I would always ask the same question: "Where is my money?" The worst part of all was the uncertainty. I had dreamed so much of making it as a professional that this ordeal became very hard to take. Things got so bad that I was forced to take a bus all the way from San Pedro to Santo Domingo and camp out at Mr. Acevedo's office. I would just be sitting there in his waiting room for hours and hours.

One morning, I remember he spotted me sitting there and said, "Wait for me here, I'll be right back." So I waited. Pretty soon it was noon. Then it was the middle of the afternoon and he was nowhere to be found. By late afternoon, his secretary told me that he called and was supposedly in Puerto Rico scouting players. He told her to tell me that I should come back another day.

I remember being so hungry that my stomach ached. At that moment, I was filled with a sense of urgency and need that was overwhelming. It was getting dark, and I didn't have the money to get back to San Pedro by bus. So I had to pawn this little gold chain I wore so I could pay for the trip. That was the only way I could get home.

Another time I went to see him, Mr. Acevedo asked me to go see a doctor friend of his so I could have a physical. When the results came back, he called me to his office and sat me down. I remember that visit like it was yesterday. He said, "I don't know what I'm going to do with you, son. The doctor doesn't think that you are going to grow very much, and to be in the big leagues, you need to have a big, strong body." I was about five feet, nine inches and a half at the time and really skinny.

What I remember about that moment was that I got angry. I said, "Look, I'm going to be a big-league ballplayer no matter what. Whether I'm big or whether I'm small. It doesn't matter. What matters is my will and my determination. So forget about this garbage that I'm too small. Whatever it takes, I'm going to get to where I need to go." I left angry. To this day I don't know why he told me that. If I hadn't had so much belief in myself that really could have hurt me.

Soon Mr. Acevedo and I went our separate ways. I thought I had been signed as a professional, but in reality I hadn't signed with anyone. My contract apparently had never been sent to the United States. I had never really been a professional, even though in my heart I was. Then I heard that Mr. Acevedo had had a falling out with the Phillies. I still don't know what happened. And he wasn't going to explain things to me because I was a nobody. But when I found out that I wasn't going to be a member of the Philadelphia Phillies, it was a really tough blow. For all the players who had been with Mr. Acevedo, there was nothing to do but look for another opportunity.

At that time, I was probably the least desirable player of Mr. Acevedo's group because the forty or so others were all older than I was and more developed physically. The scouts in

San Pedro thought those others would have a better chance than I, and some even signed contracts right away with the Atlanta Braves and other teams.

What happened to me? I didn't get any offers. But do you know what? Out of all those players, how many do you think made it to the big leagues? One. Sammy Sosa. That brings a smile to my face now, but I wasn't smiling back then. Worse still, when people in my barrio found out what had happened, some friends I thought I could count on really let me down. They said that I was a no-talent who would never reach the big leagues. It was as though my setback made them feel better about themselves.

My mother told me not to pay attention to them, and so did my brother Luis and the rest of my family. So I didn't. About the only thing I could do was to keep practicing on my own. I was back to training with Hector in the park and hitting sticks of maize in my barrio. I found out who my friends were and realized again how important my family was. They loved me no matter what.

Today, I can't say I hold any animosity to Mr. Acevedo. He was a nice person. I know that he helped me as much as he could, so I can't be ungrateful about that. What happened between us is just part of life—he had a problem he was trying to resolve, and I had a problem I was trying to resolve.

In the end, we couldn't work our problems out and had to go our separate ways. Once that happened, I didn't see him for a long time until, years later, I became aware that he had gotten very sick. As a matter of fact, he passed away about three years ago. In his dying days, he needed help so I lent him twenty-five thousand dollars so he could go to Cuba and get cancer treatments. I know for a fact that it made him very happy when I helped him. For me, it was a chance to show there were no hard feelings.

I was still only sixteen years old when I was cut loose. My

desire to make it as a professional was as intense as ever. And I still had plenty of incentives. For one, my family still didn't have enough to eat. Life was still loaded with uncertainty.

And I had a bigger problem. There were no scouts making their way to our little house to offer me a chance. I wouldn't allow myself to think my fair-weather friends in my barrio were right, so I stayed on the lookout for tryouts with other teams.

By 1985 major-league baseball was noticing that there was a great deal of talent in my country. Players like Tony Peña, George Bell, Tony Fernandez, and Alfredo Griffin were stars in the big leagues. The Toronto Blue Jays had a really famous scout on the island named Epy Guerrero who was finding kids like me, turning them into ballplayers, and filling the Blue Jays roster with Dominicans.

The Dodgers were starting to build a beautiful baseball academy where they would also start to develop many star players from the Dominican. San Pedro was full of scouts, but curiously it was said that they weren't interested in local talent. People like my friend Hector complained that it took scouts from Santo Domingo to make the journey to my town and find players like me. I didn't care who signed me as long as someone did.

Some might ask why I never held a grudge against Mr. Acevedo for what happened to me. My answer is that even though he didn't have to, he called me one day to tell me that he had arranged a tryout for me with another team. I was to report to the nearby town of San Cristóbal with my equipment and be put through a battery of drills by instructors.

By the time Mr. Acevedo had called me, I knew what these drills were like. You would have to run the sixty-yard dash, take batting practice, run in the outfield, shag flies, and show them what kind of arm you had.

My confidence was so high that I felt like I could do anything on a baseball field. I would need that faith because this tryout wasn't with just any team. This tryout was with the New York Yankees.

I made the bus ride to San Cristóbal and prepared myself for my big moment. There were a lot of other young men like me trying out in their camp, and I would have to give it my all to stand out.

I had been through a lot by the time I showed up. The Yankee instructors welcomed me to practice. Soon, I was working out with the team, going through my drills. It went well, and I began to envision myself as a Yankee. I wanted to reach the big leagues so badly it had become an obsession with me. I threw myself into every drill, and I stayed for a while, hoping that the elusive offer would finally come, that I would finally get a real contract.

"God is going to reward you," my mother told me when I left home for San Cristóbal. More than anything else back then, I hoped she was right.

This is what I looked like as a teenager (*right*) back home in the Dominican Republic, long before my dream of playing in the big leagues came true. My brother José Antonio is on the left.
PHOTO BY DR. YANILKA MORALES

Dancing with my wife, Sonia. This photo was taken at a party during a trip we took to Japan in December 1999. PHOTO BY DR. YANILKA MORALES

At the 1999 World Series with (*from left to right*) Major League Baseball Commissioner Bud Selig, home run record holder Hank Aaron, and my manager Domingo Dauhajre. PHOTO BY DR. YANILKA MORALES

My manager Domingo and I pose with Manny Ramirez (*left*) at the 1999 World Series. PHOTO BY DR. YANILKA MORALES

I had a good time meeting Japanese Prime Minister Keizo Obuchi. PHOTO BY DR. YANILKA MORALES

Alongside President Bill Clinton and my manager Domingo.
PHOTO BY DR. YANILKA MORALES

In my country, small boys begin playing baseball not long after they learn to walk. In every town and village in any part of the Dominican Republic, you'll see kids playing pickup games in the streets, in alleys, in parks and open fields with whatever they can find—a broomstick for a bat, a rock for a ball, and a tire for a backstop. PHOTO BY LYNN JOHNSON/AURORA

From April to October, Dominicans are glued to their television sets and they scan the box scores of the major league baseball season. Kids sometimes play in the shadows of satellite dishes that pull in U.S. games. PHOTO BY LYNN JOHNSON/AURORA

A picture of me as a twenty-year-old rookie with the Texas Rangers. During part of the 1989 season with the Rangers, I hit .238 with only one homer in 84 at-bats.
PHOTO BY MICHAEL PONZINI

After playing just 24 games of the 1989 season in Texas, I was traded to the Chicago White Sox in a five-player deal on July 29, 1989.
PHOTO BY MICHAEL PONZINI

I belted my 26th career home run at Comiskey Park. I had come up in the game as a pinch hitter during my disappointing 1991 season with the White Sox.
PHOTO BY MICHAEL PONZINI

I always hustled with the White Sox, but I was still very young and had to deal with shaky at-bats, strikeouts, and being sent back to the minor leagues.
PHOTO BY MICHAEL PONZINI

I was uncomfortable with the type of hitting taught by the White Sox. The team's style was to make hitters keep their heads down, weight shifted back, swing down on the ball, drop their shoulder, and release the top hand—which went against my natural swing.
PHOTO BY MICHAEL PONZINI

It's very important to keep a sense of humor during the long season.
PHOTO BY MICHAEL PONZINI

Early in my career as a Cub, the team tried many different things— including having me hit in the leadoff spot.
COURTESY OF CHICAGO CUBS/STEPHEN GREEN

Chicago is a great community where people love their sports. There is nothing like taking the field at Wrigley with thousands of Cubs fans cheering you on.
COURTESY OF CHICAGO CUBS/STEPHEN GREEN

4

"Mom, We're Millionaires!"

Everything was going well with the Yankees. I was playing well, I was practicing with their other Dominican prospects, and I was hoping to be signed. I was sixteen, and it was late 1984, a very frustrating year for me. After one practice all of the guys who were trying out for the team were in the dorm where we slept. We were all just hanging out after a practice.

I went to the bathroom in my underwear, and, as I was coming out, the cleaning lady was entering the room. I was embarassed a bit, but no big deal. It was just an accident.

The next day I went to the stadium to practice and the man who was running the Yankees camp tells me that I'm thrown off the team. Some guy who worked for him had apparently said I'd walked out of the bathroom with only my underwear on deliberately. He said to me in front of all the other players, "Take off your uniform, you're off the team."

I was stunned. In front of all the other players, I had to take off my uniform and leave. I said that his throwing me off the team was totally unjust. But he was unmoved. Then I said,

"Don't worry. You're going to see me again. I'll see you all in the big leagues."

And then I was gone from there, still without a contract. Time was going by quickly, and soon 1984 gave way to 1985 and a blur of more rejections. For example, one day I was home in San Pedro, trying to sidle up to the local scout for the Atlanta Braves. His name was Pedro Gonzalez. I was sitting near him at the ballpark, just trying to make eye contact. I'm just looking and looking and looking. But he's having a conversation with someone else, not even paying attention to me. The whole time I'm looking at him like a person looking at a plate of food when he's really hungry. That's how hungry I was.

So after a while, one of Gonzalez's employees who knew me says to him, "Pedro, this is Sammy Sosa. He was one of the players signed by Francisco Acevedo."

He studied me for a moment and said, "No, I don't sign undersized players."

I left.

Then the Montreal Expos took a look at me. At that time their scout in the Dominican was Jesus Alou, the former major leaguer whose brothers Matty and Felipe also played in the big leagues. Everyone knows now that Felipe Alou is one of the most respected managers in baseball, a source of great pride for my country because all the Alous were born and raised in the Dominican Republic. I practiced with Jesus for about two weeks. There was a small handful of us vying for one spot. But they picked another player.

Then I practiced with the New York Mets, but no one there really paid attention to me. It was always the same thing. All these scouts would see me play, they would talk about me, but it would end up being for nothing.

Later I was home talking to my mother when a friend came over to tell me that the Toronto Blue Jays wanted me to go to their training facility and practice with them. As I said earlier, in those days there was almost no protection for players like me. We had no agents or lawyers helping us and teams could keep us around as long as they wanted without offering us contracts. Today there is a lot more awareness on the island when it comes to market value and signing bonuses. But back when I was headed to train with the Blue Jays, I didn't know what to expect. Things certainly hadn't gone well up to that point.

The Blue Jays' training facility was run by a scout named Epy Guerrero who had already gained fame by sending a steady stream of other players to the big leagues and was one of the leaders in baseball's big push for players in the Dominican.

Guerrero had his own academy where he trained players in fundamentals and prepared the best of them for a trip to the United States. The Los Angeles Dodgers were competing hard with Guerrero for players. Other teams were following their leads and building baseball academies that eventually churned out talent in great numbers.

But when I got to the Blue Jays camp, it was the same old story. I practiced hard, the coaches said nice things to me, but still no contract. It was the summer of 1985. Epy Guerrero told me he wanted to sign me but that he had some other players he had to take to the United States. I had practiced hard for him, but for whatever reason he just didn't sign me. There always seemed to be more pressing priorities.

One Friday afternoon the Blue Jays were sending all of us home for the weekend. I had been practicing with the organization for a couple of months. And there were many Dominican players in Epy's facility, which was just north of Santo Domingo. I got on the bus, ready to make the two-hour ride home, with a stop in the main bus station in the capital for a transfer.

It had been more than a year since Francisco Acevedo had first "signed" me for the Phillies, but I still didn't have what I wanted—a professional contract. What I didn't know when I got on that bus was that other scouts were interested in me and had already taken steps to make contact with me before I ever reached San Pedro from the Blue Jays training camp.

To be exact, there were two scouts who were following me. Their names were Amado Dinzey and Omar Minaya, and both worked for the Texas Rangers. Minaya was a brand-new scout whom the Rangers had put in charge of scouting in my country. Dinzey worked for him. I had met Amado a few years before and had practiced with him when I was only about fourteen. I was too young then, but I would come to learn that he had been tracking me since that first encounter, right after I'd started playing organized baseball.

Amado Dinzey:

The first time I saw Sammy was in 1983. I was at the ballpark in San Pedro, watching a playoff game between two amateur teams. I didn't have a job as a scout then, but I was sitting with scouts from the Cleveland Indians and the Chicago White Sox. We were all commenting on the poor quality of players in the game when a kid walked up to us and said that he had a prospect that he knew that we all should meet.

We told the kid to bring his friend over, and who came back but Sammy Sosa. We talked with him for a while and agreed to give him a workout a few days later. That was the first time any professional scouts had ever seen him—he had never worked out for any scouts before.

He was so young at the time. After a while, we left Sammy practicing with the scout of the Chicago White Sox. But that scout took no action either. He wasn't ready yet. Later, Sammy went to the Phillies and the Yankees and went through all of that. Meanwhile, in 1984 Omar Minaya gave me a job with the Rangers, and I started looking for players they could sign. By the time I made contact with Sammy again, he was practicing with the Toronto Blue Jays.

Around this time I remember we were trying to sign a player named Bernardino Nuñez, but we lost him to the Mets. We were disappointed, but at that point I called Omar and said, "Don't worry about it, I've got a better player we can sign." At that point I started planning how we were going to get Sammy away from the Blue Jays.

Omar Minaya:

In about March 1985 I first became aware of Sammy during a conversation I had with Francisco Acevedo. Mr. Acevedo told me that Sammy was a free agent because of what had happened with the Phillies and that I should definitely see this kid. Then later I got a call from Amado, who agreed. At the time I was coaching in the Gulf Coast League in Florida, which I did for the Rangers along with scouting in the Dominican. I remember Amado said, "Listen, this kid is working out with the Toronto Blue Jays, but I think we might be able to get him."

So I arranged to fly from Sarasota, Florida, to Puerto Plata in the Dominican Republic, which is on the northern coast of the island and about three hours by bus from Santo Domingo. The Rangers used the ballpark in Puerto Plata at that time, and we tried to arrange a tryout for Sammy.

At the time there were basically no rules in scouting players in the Dominican. It was an open market, and there was a lot of competition for players. So Amado arranged for Sammy to be intercepted at the bus terminal in Santo Domingo.

Amado had a half brother in San Pedro whom he called, and he arranged for permission from Sammy's family to take Sammy to Puerto Plata. Then we intercepted him at the terminal in Santo Domingo.

Sammy Sosa:

I didn't want to go at first. I was tired, it was almost the weekend, and I had worked hard all week—I really had to think about it. But I had two friends who talked me into it. They told me that I should go. Before I agreed to go, I talked to my family as well, and they agreed that I should go. So I made the trip.

Omar Minaya:

He took the bus all the way to Puerto Plata, which was a long way. And I always tell people that the moment Sammy got off the bus, he got off swinging. You could tell that he didn't come from much, but he had a great smile, that same smile he has now. He had a great disposition, and you just had to like him. He had professionalism about him, a work ethic in everything he did.

Sammy was definitely a free swinger, but he wasn't that strong then. When he hit the ball, he would make good contact but the ball would die in the outfield. I knew what that meant. So many Dominican prospects like Sammy are malnourished by the time they reach their teens that they haven't developed physically yet. So Sammy would keep hitting that ball hard every time, but that ball would just die down every time it reached the outfield. Most of the kids we saw were not strong the first time we saw them, and you had to take that into account.

Sammy showed me a great arm, and as a scout I picked up on the fact that he had a lot of confidence in his ability. I appreciated that. But in all honesty, my first impression was that I had my doubts about Sammy. I liked him as a player, don't get me wrong. But he wasn't a fast runner. He was clocked at 7.5 seconds in the sixty-yard dash, and as a scout you are looking for players who run the sixty in at least 6.8 seconds. So I kind of wanted to sign him, but I didn't want to sign him. I was a little indecisive. That's where Amado came in and convinced me that Sammy's speed would improve.

Amado Dinzey:

Sammy's time in the sixty-yard dash was terrible for a baseball player. But I always thought that he would develop. From the time Sammy was with the Blue Jays, I was planning to lure him away. When I was able to get a hold of him, I told him he should leave Toronto.

In fact, all I did was get Sammy back after the Phillies had stolen him away. I don't know why the Blue Jays didn't want him. Probably for the same reason as Minaya—everybody here thinks players should run like racehorses.

Omar Minaya:

At one point during Sammy's workout, Amado said to me, "Omar, I know you have some concerns about his running, but with the proper training, I know he's going to get faster."

So I looked at Sammy and said, "Do you think you're going to get faster?"

In a really determined voice he said, "I will."

I said, "Okay, we'll trust you on that."

And we started negotiating right there on the spot: Amado, Sammy, and I, right there by the batting cage. That's the way they do things down there. We were offering $3,000 and he was asking for $4,000. He felt he had a market for $4,000, but what we ended up doing was splitting the difference and giving him $3,500 as a signing bonus. When it was all said and done, it was very amiable, and it took an hour and a half.

Part of being a good scout is being able to pull the trigger, and so I had one day to do it. I guess the Blue Jays weren't able to pull the trigger that fast, but that's what this business is about. We planned it from the moment Sammy got off the bus in the central station in Santo Domingo. That's why we had Amado's brother intercept him.

Sammy:

I was a professional. I had finally made it.

I went home and told my family, and we all celebrated. But this time it was going to be different from the last time. Instead of telling everyone, as I had when I signed with the Phillies, I swore my family to secrecy. When it came time, I signed the contract with the Rangers at the airport in Santo Domingo. And I did something else differently, too. This time, when the negotiations started, I didn't bring my mother. This time I told her about how it turned out when it was all over. She got a big laugh out of that. The last time, she had said, "I feel like I'm selling my son!" With her absent, this time I actually tried to negotiate with the Rangers.

In the days after I had signed, in front of my friends from the barrio I acted like nothing had changed. I kept working out in the park, and I kept hitting my pieces of maize on the street in front of my house. But little by little people began to notice that I was leaving in the morning and returning in the late afternoon. And then all of a sudden people noticed that I had money.

The Rangers' check had arrived! It was for $3,500! I remember so vividly taking the check in my hand and walking it over to my mother. She had tears in her eyes and I said, "Mom, we're millionaires!"

I was becoming who I wanted to be—a professional man, someone who could help his family. I was very dedicated to my work. It was late summer 1985, and the Rangers told me they planned to train me for a few months and then give me a chance to try out for a spot at spring training the next year. But that wouldn't be until March of 1986. I would be seventeen by then. In the meantime, I took a bus from San Pedro to Santo Domingo, where I practiced at the Olympic Center, which is right downtown. I did this five days a week, working harder than I had ever worked before. I began to visualize my dreams of being a major-league player and, most important of all, of supporting my family.

In fact, in those months before I left for the United States, I was already taking steps to make sure my family was able to eat while I was gone. Instead of spending the money on myself, I was looking for a way to invest it in something that could earn money for my family. We decided that we would take a big chunk of my $3,500 signing bonus and buy a van that my family would use as a taxi. And we did buy an older Toyota van that cost a couple thousand dollars. Even though we had the $3,500, we were still very poor, and I felt that burden. The taxi was a way of easing that burden.

Buying the van was my first business decision. (Well, my second, if you include my negotiations with Texas.) And like a lot of important decisions in my life, I talked it over with my friend Bill Chase.

Bill Chase:

When Sammy signed with the Rangers, I didn't think he would ever be a star, but I thought he could make the big leagues. And in the time leading up to his signing, Sammy and his brother Jose Antonio had grown so close to my wife and me that they were spending the weekends at our house in Santo Domingo. Every Friday night they would ride on the bus with us from San Pedro to Santo Domingo, and we'd take them out to eat.

But first, both of the boys would take a two-hour shower. I'm not exaggerating. It was like their weekly shower, and we'd have to pry them out of there because we'd be getting really hungry waiting for them. We always ate at a place right on the oceanside in Santo Domingo, along what the Dominicans call the Malecón.

The restaurant was called La Parilla, and we always ate with a bunch of Americans who lived in Santo Domingo. Then, on Saturday nights during the baseball season, we'd take them to a ball game. Jose Antonio would always stay with us because he was still kind of young. But I wouldn't see Sammy from the time we got there until the time we were ready to go—he would go hang out with the guys.

From the time Sammy was fourteen this had become like a ritual. Whatever the boys wanted, they got. And all this time it was like helping their family survive. My wife and I had set up a fund to help Sammy's family. It wasn't big, but they were probably going to get about $100 a week out of it. And then all of a sudden, Sammy signed the Phillies contract, which I didn't know about. That was okay, he certainly didn't have to tell me everything. At this point I was always helping the kids, giving them a little something extra so they could help out their family.

Then after Sammy signed his contract with the Rangers, he came up to me and asked if he could borrow some money to buy this van. For the first time in his life, I turned him down. I said, "Don't spend your money on that. You're not going to have time to run it. It's not going to work and you're going to lose all your money." But Sammy went ahead and bought the van.

Sammy:

For a long time I had asked Bill for things and he had always been there to help my family. We would always ask and then wait to hear whether he said yes or no. The van was important because of our financial situation. Before I left for the United States, I even drove it myself as a taxi around the streets of my town.

Around the same time, I bought myself another blue bicycle and was riding it all over the barrio. I was really happy with my success and decided to myself that I wanted to find someone to share it with.

So I got on my bike and went looking for a girlfriend. At this point in my life I was still a barrio kid and sporting an Afro. I went up to one young lady I knew and asked her if she would be my girlfriend. She said no. I went up to another one—same answer. I approached a third—rejected again. A fourth—get lost.

Then I rode my bike over and asked a fifth girl the same question that had gotten me nothing but rejection. The answer was the same. No. I guess they didn't think I would ever amount to anything. They were judging me by the way I looked. I suppose they weren't very impressed with my blue bicycle. I decided there was nothing I could do but keep going in the direction God was pointing me. My faith was stronger than ever.

I thought, "I'm just going to keep pushing forward." And I did.

By the time 1986 rolled around, I knew the big moment was coming—my chance to finally make it to the United States and go after my dream of being a major-league ballplayer. And just as he always had, Bill was helping me again.

He had given me a set of dumbbells and barbells to improve my upper-body strength. They weren't Nautilus or fancy or anything, but I used them every day. Bill had told me that I would see American players who were a lot bigger than I was and that I needed to build up my upper body and my legs. For my legs, he said, "Run on the beach until your legs ache." So I did. Every day, I ran as hard as I could. And I was making progress. Omar Minaya would tell me later that he was amazed at how fast I was developing in such a short period. I was running faster and growing stronger. The Rangers were paying for my transportation in and out of Santo Domingo and my meals.

Then in February of 1986 came the big test. The Rangers had arranged a key practice where they would evaluate their Dominican talent and decide who would go to spring training. This wasn't just any other practice. Sandy Johnson, who was director of scouting for the Rangers at that time, had flown to Santo Domingo to observe the practice himself. Sandy didn't know who I was and had never seen me before. But I wasn't nervous because of what was at stake. I believed in myself.

I was in right field, shagging fly balls and throwing hard into the infield. The coaches told me that Sandy was surprised by what he saw. He didn't know what to expect and was really impressed with my arm strength.

Then he saw me hit the ball, and I hit it very well. Because of the work I was doing with my barbells, my hits weren't dying in the shallow outfield anymore. They were traveling.

I was doing my work when all of a sudden, Sandy called me over to him. I'll never forget what he said: "When you're in the big leagues, I don't want you to be a hothead like Ruben Sierra because you are going to be better than he is." At that time Ruben was one of the top prospects in the Rangers system. He was a Puerto Rican right fielder who went on to have great years in the late 1980s and early 1990s. In 1989, in fact, he almost won the American League MVP. Ruben was also known as being hot-tempered, and I guess Sandy was trying to give me a message because he could see that on the field I was an aggressive player.

The practice was soon over and I went home.

I was still helping my family with the van, but our taxi venture was becoming a problem. The van kept breaking down, and we weren't making much money off it. Between that and other expenses, all my signing bonus money was gone. So I was praying for a chance, hoping that I had made a good enough impression to earn a spot at spring training. If I didn't make it, I would have to spend the summer playing against other developing Dominican prospects. Nobody in my position wanted to do that. Everybody wanted to go to the United States.

Then I realized once again what my mother always told me—that life brings both blessings and challenges.

We eventually sold the van—for a hundred dollars. Before it was all said and done, it had become a major distraction and something that upset my family very much. Important people who have known me like Bill Chase and Omar Minaya know what a problem that van became in my life.

They would tell me that the distraction and money worries it caused would show on my face and weigh on me because in those early years I felt the responsibility of caring for my family so much. I felt like my family was in my hands, so I wanted to do everything I could for them.

But what gave me hope were the blessings that were coming my way. Word came from the Rangers that I was going to America!

The team had purchased a plane ticket for me that would leave Santo Domingo, go through Miami, and connect to Plant City, Florida, the Rangers' spring training site.

I had never seen such excitement around my house. My mother and my family members put their money together and planned a farewell party for me. It was wonderful. And then we prepared for the big day, when my whole family accompanied me to Santo Domingo's International Airport for my first trip to the United States—in fact, my first trip anywhere.

I remember being more excited that day than I had ever been before. I was happy, too, because I wasn't going alone. Two friends of mine—Billy Wilson and Jose Concepcion— would be making the trip with me. It would also be my first time on an airplane.

But while I was excited, my mother wasn't. We had never been separated before. Her strength was always having her children near her. By the time my big day came, we had been through so much together. I thought about all of our moments together on that morning I left—all the moments my family and I had shared, how we had survived together and grown as close as a family could be.

Whenever she tells this story, it still brings tears to her eyes.

Mireya Sosa:

I don't like to remember that day. I cried so much. I had always had my kids with me, and now my Mikey was leaving. I was crying and crying. We were all there and I hugged Mikey and said, "Son, I wish you didn't have to leave. I love you so much."

Sammy:

I told her not to worry. I kept saying, "Mom, I'm leaving now, but I'm going to come back."

I said goodbye to all my brothers and sisters, but I could see how much this was hurting my mother.

Mireya Sosa:

He went to get on the plane, and I watched him. Through the window I could see him get on. He looked through his seat window and smiled. Then he gave me the thumbs-up signal. All I was doing was crying.

The plane began to pull away with my son on it, and then it was gone. I just stood there watching it as it took off. My other children were ready to go but I wasn't. Not yet.

The rest of the family began to get restless. One of them said, "Come on, Mom. Let's go."

I said, "Wait." And through the window, I watched as the plane got smaller and smaller in the distance. I couldn't leave until it was completely gone.

I suffered a great deal in those first months when Sammy left. I understood that he was fulfilling his destiny, but it broke my heart to see him leave.

Sammy had always provided me with so much strength— he had always been such a good son and such a good brother. So I just stood there until I couldn't see the plane any longer. Then it was time to leave.

He was gone.

5

The Fragile Years

So there I was on the plane, as excited as I could be. I don't remember much about the ride, but I do remember what happened once we got there. The plane was coming in for a landing at Miami International Airport and was full of people. The pilot landed the plane okay, and then we came to a stop—but we were still on the runway.

I have flown hundreds of times since then, so I now know that you must remain seated until the plane has come to a complete stop at the gate. You can always tell by that familiar chime telling you to grab your belongings and go.

Well, there I was, never having traveled before and not knowing that we hadn't gotten to the gate yet. So me and another friend, Felipe Castillo, who was sitting next to me, just unbuckled our seat belts, got up, and started grabbing our bags from the overhead compartment.

All of a sudden, I noticed that everyone was staring at us and that the flight attendants were telling us—in English—to sit down. I said, *"Felipe, que pasa?"*

And he said, "Damn, I thought we were here."

It still makes me laugh when I think about it because he

said it in such a funny way. We were still standing up when the plane started moving again, so we sat down as fast as we could, but it was too late. Everyone was looking at us like we were crazy. That was my first experience in the United States.

The next thing I knew we were at the gate and there was a person saying welcome to Miami in both English and Spanish. "Welcome to Miami and its beaches!"

We had to catch a connecting flight to Plant City, which, as we discovered, was all the way at the other end of the airport. By the time we cleared customs and got our bags, we were running late and barely made our flight.

We didn't arrive in Plant City until late that night. Once we got to the hotel I was really tired, but I remember looking around and thinking, "What a beautiful hotel." I don't remember exactly where we stayed, but it was a far cry from the palatial hotels I stay in now as a big leaguer. But to me, at that time, that hotel was like a palace.

Within a day or so we were working out with all the Rangers' prospects and getting used to their system of doing things. The team would feed us in the morning and then again around four in the afternoon. After that you were on your own. If you had some money, you would go buy yourself a pizza or go to McDonald's or something. I remember that was a really hard situation for me because a lot of times I didn't have any money—I was sending most of my $700-a-month salary to my family. And that meant that a lot of times by seven or eight at night, I'd be starving. We were working really hard, and my body was growing, and it seemed like I was always hungry. So during team meals I would eat a lot and then stuff food in my pockets that I would then take back to my hotel room to eat later.

In the minor leagues during training camp—and during regular season—a bunch of guys would live together in the same place to cut down on expenses. During that first spring training, I was with my friends Billy Wilson, Angelo Encarnacion, and a few other players. All of us were always short on money, especially me.

Not long after I arrived in Plant City, I had a money problem that really hurt. I was saving this little stash of forty dollars that I had brought with me to the United States, practically guarding it with my life.

At the same time I was still getting used to the Rangers' system of doing things. One thing was the laundry. All the players were instructed to throw their laundry in a hamper, and it would get done. Well, I threw a pair of pants in there, but I'd forgotten that I'd left my wallet in the back pocket. So the pants got thrown in the washing machine—wallet, forty dollars, and all. The money was completely lost!

At that time it was a disaster, because I had lost the only money I had!

So there I was playing baseball, not knowing how to speak a word of English. I didn't know anything. I had to ask people to do everything, even the simplest tasks. All of us Dominican players would have to get up earlier than the other players to catch the bus to the stadium because we were always worried about making a mistake and arriving late. But when you have the need to be somebody, you don't let those things get you down. And I had the need to be someone. The road is a difficult one, and I say "is" because it's not over yet. The road for me continues.

But at that time all of us Latin players had something hanging over our heads when we first arrived in America for spring training. We didn't, under any circumstances, want to get sent back to the Dominican. There was a summer league there back then—not like the one they have today, which all Dominicans have to play in before going to the States. Back in 1986 that league was for the rejects, the players who couldn't cut it in the United States and needed more work.

I knew guys who were so afraid of being sent back that they were ready to bolt to New York and stay in the States illegally rather than go back home. Believe me, we didn't want to go back!

So I worked really, really hard. I took outfield practice constantly. And what I remember about the first practice sessions was how amazed I was. I would look around and think, "Damn, these American players are big." I would be standing among them in the outfield, and they would seem huge. I was developing physically, but my background compared to theirs wasn't the same nutritionally, and it showed. They all seemed really strong, and I was still very thin.

But during batting practice I noticed that I was hitting the ball a lot better than they were. That gave me hope. Toward the end of that first camp, I was doing everything I could to demonstrate to the Americans that I should stay.

Along with some of the Dominican players I knew from back home, Omar Minaya was there as well. And I learned that if I stayed in the United States, and was sent to the Rookie League in Sarasota, Florida, Omar would be there, too, as an instructor and as a big brother to the Latin players on the team.

Today a lot of big-league teams use this system. They hire Spanish-speaking coaches who not only help Latin players during instruction but also can help them in the equally important matter of adjusting to life in the United States. That was a big challenge for all the Latin guys, and Omar was there to help.

Omar Minaya:

At that stage of his life, Sammy was a very happy person; there was a lot of positive energy in his smile and his mannerisms. He was a focused kid with an eagerness to understand this new culture that he had been thrown into. I remember as soon as Sammy got to spring training, we challenged him. Right away we put him in against triple-A players to see what he could do, and he would handle it.

I remember watching him hit a double in that first game against triple-A competition. Now at that time, Ruben Sierra was just about to make the scene in the big leagues, and so here was Sammy trying to compete against Ruben. And people kind of started saying, "Who is this guy?"

Because of his aggressiveness and his confidence, he acted like he belonged, like his time was coming.

Around this time there was another player who just arrived named Juan Gonzalez. The amazing thing about these two guys was that the first time they met, they kind of gravitated to each other, and pretty soon they were in the outfield playing catch. The first time they played catch professionally, they played with each other—Sammy Sosa and Juan Gonzalez! But you have to remember that at that point, they still faced a long road to the major leagues. Yet you could tell the talent was there.

Sammy had improved his running speed, his overall strength, and his throwing arm. Juan was a sixteen-year-old kid from Puerto Rico and was kind of in the same boat as Sammy. He was maybe a little more advanced because up to that point, he had played in more organized baseball than Sammy.

Organized baseball in San Pedro de Macorís is not that well organized or coached, so Sammy was truly a diamond in the rough. We knew it was a matter of making sure Sammy was focused and helping him as much as possible in removing problems that would distract him from baseball.

The one thing Sammy had to deal with that the other players didn't was a large amount of stress. After all, he had to provide for his family on his salary. That was very difficult. So I tried to make sure that I always had a little extra money for him and made sure he had the confidence to know that he could come to me.

Sammy has always been able to show his emotions, and you could always tell if he had a problem—it would be all over his face. He was always wondering if his family was taken care of. Right after he got to America, his stepfather got sick, and that happened right after the business venture had gone bad. So Sammy was always saving a dollar and sending a dollar home to his mother.

For a Latin player, those first years in the United States are the fragile years. A lot of kids don't make it. (Editor's note: Some 90 to 95 percent of foreign-born baseball prospects are released at the class-A level.)

So Sammy would be pulling his money together, and every now and then he would ask me for an extra twenty bucks here or another twenty there. After a while, I came to know that Sammy was the type of kid who would always help out if he found someone on the street worse off than him. I always thought he was very admirable that way.

Sammy:

We were coming to the end of spring training, and, as I said, I was getting worried. A lot of times, especially when you're first starting out, you don't know where you stand in baseball—you don't know what plans they have for you.

That's how I was feeling when the day came to choose which players would stay and which would be sent home. The Rangers had this big bulletin board, and they told us they were going to put all the names of the players who made it on the board. If your name wasn't there, it meant you were going home.

So when the day came, I and my friends all ran up to the board and pushed our way to the front. All the players were there, and there was all this screaming and yelling. I was frantic, scanning up and down to find my name somewhere—*anywhere!*

I looked up. I looked down. I couldn't see it. My friends were yelling, "Where is my name? Where is my name?"

My friend Billy Wilson was there with me. Billy is Dominican, but he has an Anglo name because his ancestors were from the island of Antigua. As I looked for my name, he had a horrible realization. He hadn't gotten picked. They were sending him back to the Dominican.

He was really upset, and so was I. I was really sad for him. My friend Billy would refuse to go back to the Dominican.

He said he was going to quit the team and go to New York. I tried to talk him out of it. I said, "Billy, don't quit. You're really talented. You can make the big leagues." But he was so upset he didn't listen to me. He left.

It was very upsetting because Billy and my friend Jose Concepcion had always been true friends, the kind of friends who fill you full of confidence, who encourage you to move forward, and who tell you not to take anything from anyone. I never forgot that or them.

So on that day I felt sad for Billy, but I felt blessed as well. How did I discover my blessing?

After not being able at first to find my name, I suddenly saw a flash that lifted my spirits. Right there. At the very bottom of the last page. In tiny little letters. There was a beautiful sight for my eyes. It was just one word. SOSA. *Oh my God!* I was staying in the United States.

The Rangers would be sending me to Daytona Beach,

Florida, for what they called "extended" spring training, which is just what it sounds like: an extended training session that all teams have for their absolute beginners like me. We would practice in Daytona from the end of March until June and then be sent to Sarasota for Rookie League play. The Rookie League season is always the shortest because it's filled with young teenagers like me taking their first steps in professional baseball.

And let me tell you, we had quite an assemblage of talent. Yes, I was competing against some guys who would not only reach the big leagues but also would become stars and, in a few cases, superstars.

On that one Rookie League team in 1986, the Rangers had both me and Juan Gonzalez. Juan, of course, went on to win the American League MVP in 1996 and 1998.

At third base we had Dean Palmer, who had just graduated from high school in Tallahassee, Florida, and, so far, has had four big-league seasons of more than 30 home runs and three 100-plus RBI seasons.

At shortstop we had Rey Sanchez, from Rio Piedras, Puerto Rico, one of the guys I used to pal around with a lot. It was Rey's first year in professional baseball, too, and a bunch of us used to spend our off time going to McDonald's.

Rey has been a solid big-league shortstop for almost ten years now and played really well for us that year in Sarasota, hitting .290.

And our star pitcher was the Rangers' number-one draft pick in 1986, a right-hander who threw so hard that nobody wanted to take batting practice against him. Except me. His name was Kevin Brown. I remember when I first saw him, I noticed that he had this incredible sinker. Even back then, he was a gamer. In fact, the way he is now—intimidating and tough—is the way he was back then. But I wasn't intimidated.

I loved challenges. And I remember hitting a couple of his pitches off the wall.

Being a top draft choice from America, Kevin lived a different life from me back then. His life was about Corvettes and a lot of money in bonuses. As a Latin player, you're aware of the differences between you and the Americans, but you never let it get in the way of what you have to do.

Kevin didn't stay with us very long that summer. After three games with us in Sarasota, the Rangers moved him up really fast. They sent him to double-A Tulsa, a huge jump, and then took him all the way to the big club to finish the 1986 season.

I wanted to move up really fast, too, and thought I could. When we got to Daytona Beach, I remember that I wanted to play class-A ball. I thought I was ready for that. A person knows when he can do something, and I was hitting well. But they didn't pick me for A ball. They said I was too young and that I wasn't mature enough. I had to be patient, which wasn't easy for me.

I remember that during this time, we were getting to know Daytona and, by extension, America. When we first got there, the team took us to this Chinese restaurant that was an all-you-can-eat kind of place. During extended spring training Sunday was our only day off, so we would go there—Felipe Castillo, Rey Sanchez, Juan Gonzalez and I.

I remember the owner couldn't believe how much we could eat. And after a while, he'd see us coming and yell, "No, no. No ballplayers. No ballplayers. *You eat too much!*"

Because we Latin guys didn't have a car, all we could ever do for entertainment was to walk to the beach, which was right across the street from our hotel. We would always go to the beach. When it came time to move to Sarasota, all of us moved into the same little apartment, along with another player named Mickey Cruz.

We all lived together and did everything together. People often ask me how it was to play with Juan Gonzalez. I say it was great. He was and always has been a really good person. To his friends Juan is known as Igor, a nickname he picked up in Puerto Rico. And even then I could tell he was going to be a great player. For the next three seasons, we came up the ranks together. When the two of us started playing in real games, it wasn't long before we were being noticed.

But, as always during those early years, my thoughts were often with my family and how things were going at home. During my first year in the minor leagues, my mother got sick, and I became desperate to hear from her.

Mireya Sosa:

I had circulation problems in my legs and was feeling very ill. I was also missing Sammy terribly. I hadn't spoken to him in a while and felt terrible about that. Then, one day, as a surprise my family arranged to talk to him. Amado Dinzey came by and said, "You have to talk to your son. He's back in Florida worried about you, and he's just beside himself." When Sammy came on the phone, I couldn't stop my tears.

He said, "Mom, are you crying?"

I said, "They are tears of happiness, it's so good to hear your voice."

We talked on the phone for about an hour and a half. He asked about his brothers and sisters and how everyone was doing. I've been blessed because he's always kept me close to his heart. I felt so much better after I spoke with him. I got better physically, and they told me later that after our talk he went out and hit a home run!

Sammy:

In sixty-one games that year in Sarasota I hit four home runs. The Rangers didn't project me as a home-run hitter back then. My main attribute was, curiously, my speed, which had increased a lot since I started working out professionally. That first year in the minors I hit .275 with four home runs and 28 RBI. I stole 11 bases, and I led my league in doubles with 19. Juan and I were taking our first steps. He hit .240. He didn't hit any home runs, but he had 36 RBI. We were showing the Rangers flashes of the talent we had inside of us.

Omar Minaya:

Sammy was developing. He was definitely separating himself from the other players. By the end of that first Rookie League season, we thought that Sammy and Juan had the potential to be above-average major-league players.

Sammy:

For my first year in Rookie League, I had a productive season, I did a good job. The Rangers kept me in the United States after the season playing instructional-league ball. After that I went home in the fall.

I was thrilled to see my mother and my brothers and sisters. But when I came home to the Dominican after that first year in the United States, everything looked different to me. It's like I wasn't the same kid from the barrio anymore. I was making money. And all of a sudden, I saw my mom and siblings with different eyes: they looked so thin to me! I would look at Jose Antonio and say, "My brother, you're so skinny!" I had brought them clothes from the States, and money. People looked at me differently, too. My clothes were nicer, and I had cut my hair.

Mireya Sosa:

When I saw Sammy, I couldn't believe my son looked so beautiful, so handsome.

Sammy:

I think some of the girls in the neighborhood were thinking that I would come back wearing short pants like I used to, but I had matured. I felt like I was glowing. Like I was different. Like I was better.

"The man is changing," people said to me. Others would say, "Man, look at him."

In those days the rapper L. L. Cool J was really popular. I liked him so much that I bought a pair of red shoes and wrote "L. L. Cool J" on them. And then I wore them when I went home.

The next year, 1987, the Rangers sent me to a lower-level class-A team in Gastonia, a small town in western North Carolina. I felt a lot more experienced when I arrived, like I had traveled and knew my way around.

I was trying to learn English as best I could by speaking with my American teammates. Sometimes they would have a little fun with me. Like the first "word" they taught me: "cometomyroom." They also taught me how to say, "You are so beautiful." I would say it, "bee-you-tee-full."

I was asking a lot of questions by this point. I was always asking, "How do you say this? Or how do you say that?" I wanted to learn because I wanted to be able to do things for myself. Going out to eat was still hard because I couldn't order for myself. I would go out with my American friends and stand next to them as they ordered their food. Then, when my friends would order, I would say, "Like that," which meant that I often didn't get to eat what I wanted but had to eat the same as the guy I was with.

After a while, I would wear my American teammates out with my questions. They would say, "Sosa, I'm tired!" Or, "Sosa, shut up!"

I really wanted to do more things for myself because I had always been self-reliant. One day, during my second spring in America, Felipe Castillo and I went to a supermarket in Daytona Beach. We were really hungry for some Dominican food, so we decided we were going to buy some tuna and prepare it with onions the way they do back home. So we're at the store buying food, and we get the tuna—or what we think is tuna. Now keep in mind that Felipe and I could barely speak English at this point and couldn't really read it. So back at the apartment we opened the cans, sliced some onions, and we were just to about to eat when some older guys from the team, guys who had been around a little longer than Felipe and I, showed up. We talked for a little bit and then got ready to start eating. As I had the fork in my hands, one of the guys grabs me and yelled, *"Don't!"* I looked at him like he was crazy. But then he told me why he stopped me. "Man, this isn't tuna. This is cat food!" We almost ate cat food! It was like, welcome to America!

Lucikly, things were going better for me on the field. Juan and I were in the outfield together in Gastonia, and we were destroying the league. Wilson Alvarez, a promising left-handed pitcher from Venezuela, had joined our team. Dean Palmer was with us as well.

We had a lot of camaraderie. Things were great. Both Juan and I got picked to play in the South Atlantic League All-Star Game, which was in Knoxville, Tennessee, that year. I remember the owner of the team took us in his car, and we had a really good time.

A bunch of us guys were living together in Gastonia, and we would all take turns cooking, or we would eat at McDonald's. It was also a good year because I got to see Bill Chase pretty regularly that season. He had a shoe factory he owned in South Carolina, so he would come to the States on business and drive up to see me in Gastonia. It was great to see someone from home.

Bill Chase:

The year Sammy played in Gastonia, I realized that he could definitely make the big leagues. I knew before then—I had a gut feeling—but in Gastonia I was convinced. I used to find a reason to go to my finishing factory in South Carolina and then drive the forty minutes to Gastonia to see Sammy.

At that point Sammy was still only about 165 pounds and skinny as a rail—his basic assets were speed and fielding. When I would visit, all the Spanish-speaking players were living together—about five or six guys—so they could cut costs.

So after games I would offer to take all of them out to dinner, which was easy because the only place they ever went was McDonald's. There would be Sammy, Juan Gonzalez, Rey Sanchez, Wilson Alvarez, all the other kids, and I.

It was tough for Sammy during those years—tough for all those kids. But Sammy always had the one asset it took to be great: guts. He had the drive and the willpower. He just wasn't going to take second best.

Sammy:

I had a good year in Gastonia. I hit .279 with 11 home runs and 59 RBI. Juan hit .265 with 14 home runs and 74 RBI. From that moment on, he and I were always ranked as the top two prospects in the Rangers' organization. Sometimes I'd be ranked number one and he'd be ranked number two, and then he'd be number one and I'd be number two.

I played in instructional league again that year and went home feeling great. I came back the next year and they put me in the Florida State League, which was a really tough league. It was the highest level of class-A ball. This was 1988, and I was nineteen.

It was a hard year, but I learned a lot, about myself and about baseball. Omar Minaya was still close by. He and I talked a lot.

Omar Minaya:

Sammy's stats that year weren't very good. He only hit .229, and Juan only hit .256. But I really feel Sammy was blessed that he went to the Texas Rangers system because the Rangers were developing a lot of Latin players. They were doing that because they were very understanding of the Latin player. Sandy Johnson, who was the director of scouting, understood that you had to be more patient with the Latin players, that they sometimes take a little longer to develop.

Sammy was a young player, a very aggressive one who knew one thing: he had to perform. And when he got the Florida State League, he was playing against guys who were older than he was, who were further along in their development. So when he started struggling, we thought, "That's okay, we don't need him to be great. We need him to learn." And most of all with a player like Sammy, we didn't want to take away his individuality. He struck out 106 times that year, but in all honesty, one of the things I kept reinforcing was to keep swinging.

He needed to develop that comfort and philosophy at the plate. He had the ability to do things instinctively, but when you're that way at a young age, you are going to make mistakes. And he did. It was then that he became known for swinging at a lot of bad pitches. But I knew it would just be a matter of time before he improved on his pitch identification.

It was during this time that Sammy began to have some trouble with his coaches, because some of them sensed that "you can't mess with Sammy because he has backers." If Sammy had trouble, he could just pick up the phone and call me, and I think there was kind of a backlash against that. To be truthful, it was a little bit on the racial side. In baseball, as in all sports, first-round draft choices get special treatment. But unfortunately, when a Latin kid has special treatment, it's a problem. Some coaches think, "Here is a kid who doesn't even speak English, and I have to treat him like a number-one pick?"

That was one of the keys, too. It's a racial mindset that here is a Latin kid who has a godfather or is protected by the system like he is a number-one pick.

And I always encouraged Sammy to be opinionated. I told him, "Don't be a yes man." Some coaches in the late 1980s weren't used to that. But Sandy Johnson had told me, "You let me know if there are problems with Sammy because we are going to protect him." That would piss people off.

Sammy:

Even though I hit .229, I stole 42 bases that year and led the league in triples. My game was getting more explosive, and my confidence was growing. When I went back to the Dominican after the season, I really wanted to play in the Dominican Winter League. I was contracted to play for the team Escogido, a really famous team in my country, and I showed up at the stadium ready to play.

Phil Regan was the manager. He is a good man, and he gave me a chance. He started putting me in games. By this time I was really fast and could go from first to third on a single. And after a while, it seemed like every time they would put me in a game, we would win!

I was a happy man. But I wasn't starting a lot. They had me coming off the bench, so I went to the owner and said, "Come on, put me in games. I didn't come here just to run. I can hit. I can field." They tried to explain to me that I was still young, but I said, "Look, not even Jose Canseco can take right field away from me!" I smile now when I think about that, but you have to be confident to be a ballplayer, especially at this level. There is so much competition.

At this point I thought, "I'm going to fight and compete against anybody. Nobody is going to take my job away from me." And when I said that, it was like God said, "Amen," because from then on I was starting.

I hit .270 and was second in the league in RBI. I was named the league's rookie of the year, my team won the league championship, and we went to Mazatlán, Mexico, for the Caribbean World Series.

I had just turned twenty and had only been playing baseball seriously since I was fourteen. But I was developing into Sammy Sosa. Suddenly I was a prospect, and people were treating me differently. Things were starting to come my way, and I was happy that I had people to share it with.

Bill Chase:

By the time Sammy was playing for Escogido, I had this Daihatsu that we used like a company car—a nice little thing, turbo-charged; my wife and I used it. We also had a van we were using, so I told Sammy that while he was back in the Dominican, he could use the Daihatsu. Well, all of a sudden it seemed to be his.

We used to go to Santo Domingo to watch him play. Sammy would get us tickets, but it was different than the will-call system here. In the Dominican you had to go to the back of the stadium and pound on the gate. Then somebody would come out, and you'd say that Sammy had left you tickets. At that point they'd go and get Sammy, and he would bring the tickets. One time we showed up for a game, but Sammy hadn't arrived yet. So we were waiting for him when I heard this music just pounding from three miles away.

My wife said, "I bet that's Sammy."

And I said, "Nah." Sure enough, here comes Sammy in that little Daihatsu, but he had had speakers installed in it that were bigger than the car. And painted on the door of the car were the words: SAMMY SOSA.

It still makes me laugh when I think about it.

Sammy:

I was feeling great. And by the time the Caribbean World Series was over there was even better news. The Rangers were inviting me to their major-league spring training. For the first time I would fly first-class like the real big leaguers. I would earn big-league meal money and stay in the big hotel.

There was no guarantee that I would make the team; in fact, most people were saying that it was just a tune-up for the big time, that I would be sent to double-A for more seasoning. I didn't care. I was one step closer to the big leagues, and nobody was going to stand in my way.

By surviving the Florida State League and having a breakthrough season in winter ball and then getting invited to the big-league camp, I felt like I had cleared a hurdle.

I was on my way.

6

The Call

By the time I arrived in Florida for my first spring training with big-league players, I was in a whole other world. Suddenly agents and lawyers started flocking around me. I had never gotten that kind of attention before, but their interest was a reaction to the faith the Rangers had in me.

I didn't know what I should do or who I should choose. A lot of people were making a lot of promises to me. So the Rangers helped me out a little bit with finding the right person to represent me. Luis Rosa—a really famous scout in Latin America—had signed Juan Gonzalez for the Rangers and got involved in helping me find an agent. At that time Luis was the best scout there was. Before working for the Rangers, Luis had been a scout for the San Diego Padres and filled their roster with some of the best Latin talent available: Benito Santiago, Carlos Baerga, Ozzie Guillen, Sandy Alomar Jr., and Robby Alomar. All of those guys became all-stars. The Padres traded or lost all of them, but it wasn't Luis's fault.

And Luis wasn't done. He had a fuzzy-cheeked, pudgy little catcher from Vega Baja, Puerto Rico, in camp. His name was Ivan Rodriguez, and that "pudgy" appearance got him his nickname, Pudge.

The Rangers thought so much of Pudge that they didn't even send him to Sarasota for Rookie League as they had done for Juan and me. He went straight to Gastonia, and two years later, before he had even turned twenty, Pudge was in the big leagues. He's been there ever since. But I didn't see too much of him that spring because he was over with the minor leaguers.

Anyway, Luis Rosa was helping me find an agent. I could tell he was really helping Juan, too, and I think he sent him to Scott Boras or somebody really big. He then had a conversation with an agent named Adam Katz. Luis said, "I can't give you Juan Gonzalez, but I have a little ballplayer I want you to represent." I was like a cheap gift they were giving away. And that's how I got Adam Katz as my agent. He still works with me.

By the spring of 1989, in the shape I was in, I thought that had I been born in the United States, I would have gotten lots of money to sign a contract. By then I could hit, run, and throw. I've seen lots of players from the United States, top draft choices who got lots of money, and that would have been me, too.

But don't get me wrong. I'm not complaining about being born in the Dominican. I'm proud of who I am, and I love my country. But there is a difference in how talent is purchased. I've used that difference like so many other things in my life—as motivation. And what motivated me even more that spring was the talent on the Rangers team. I knew I had to fight hard just to get on that roster. There were a lot of great players, many of them from Latin America. Rafael Palmeiro had just come over to the team in a trade from the Chicago Cubs and would play first base.

By this time Ruben Sierra had broken through and was

poised to have a fantastic season that year—he batted .306, with 29 home runs. He led the league in RBI, with 119; he also led the league in triples, with 14; and in slugging percentage, with .543. And he played a great right field—the position I wanted. In 1988 Ruben had driven in more than 90 runs, and the year before he had 109 RBI. At twenty-three, only three years older than I was, Ruben was already at the top of his game and a rising star.

Also on that team was my countryman Julio Franco, another great hitter. Julio had just come to the Rangers in a trade from the Cleveland Indians. By the time he got to camp, Julio had already had three consecutive seasons of hitting .300 or better. He would make it four years in a row in 1989 by hitting .316 with 92 RBI. Two years later, in 1991, Julio hit .341 and won the American League batting championship. Julio is from San Pedro de Macorís and was already in the big leagues when I was just starting to play organized ball in the sandlots of our hometown. That spring Julio took me under his wing and showed me around. He knew how badly I wanted to make the big leagues and how much I wanted to play right field for the Rangers.

He might have even known something about Ruben Sierra because when I showed up, I had a notion to tell Ruben that he had better get ready to play center field because I was going to take over in right. I was young.

Anyway, Julio got wind of how I was feeling and wasn't above having some fun. He would look over at Ruben and whisper to me, "Tell him, tell him, tell him." He wanted me to tell Ruben that I would take his job away from him. Julio was really egging me on. So I did it. I said, "Ruben, you better start getting used to center field because right field is mine." I told him as a joke—I was just having fun with him.

But people like Omar Minaya heard what I said, and to them it showed that I had a lot of confidence. What they were also noticing that spring was that my game was improving, that it had really benefited from the hard-earned experience I'd gotten in the previous two years.

Omar Minaya:

I still remember Sammy talking to Ruben. Ruben told him, "Hey, you're going to be a good center fielder."

And Sammy said, "Nah, nah, nah. I'm going to be the right fielder—you're going to have to play center."

But all kidding aside, when Sammy first got to the major-league spring training in 1989 and got up against those major leaguers, that was the moment you could see he was going to be an all-star. When he got up there, he just stood out so much. Then you started thinking, "Wow. This guy looks like Clemente." The aura of Roberto Clemente came to people's minds when Sammy ran. You could see he was going to be special.

Sammy:

By this point in my life, I was getting something I had never gotten before—attention in the press. Before spring training started, I was starting to get written about in the bigger newspapers. The word about me was good. Phil Regan, my manager at Escogido and at that time an advance scout with the Dodgers, said in the *Dallas Morning News,* "Sammy is the most improved player I've seen [in the Dominican Winter League]. On two-strike situations he's shortened up his stroke and put the ball in play. And with his speed, that's all he needs to do." That spring the *Dallas Morning News* also wrote,

> The biggest debate among scouts who watch the Rangers play is who will be the better big leaguer—Juan Gonzalez or Sammy Sosa. Sosa doesn't have Gonzalez's power, but he'll hit a few home runs. He has as much speed as anybody in the organization and has a rifle arm. . . . There is no doubting Sosa's desire to play and his willingness to work.

Then, late in the spring, Blackie Sherrod, also of the *Dallas Morning News,* wrote, "Sammy Sosa remains the best young prospect in the Rangers organization—best speed, best arm, best hitting eyes."

Although I was playing really well against the big-league players, most people were saying that I would start the year in Tulsa, with the Rangers' double-A team. No one wanted to rush me, and there was a strong sense of optimism in the Rangers organization. So it was decided that I would start the 1989 season in Tulsa, in the Texas League.

I accepted the decision and arrived in Oklahoma ready to destroy the league. And that's what Juan and I did. In fact, I don't have that many memories of living in Tulsa because I was so focused on getting to the big leagues and proving that I belonged in Arlington, Texas, not Tulsa, Oklahoma. By late May, I was hitting over .300 and was in the top ten in league batting average. In fact, during one fantastic week Juan had the third-highest batting average, I had the fifth, and Dean Palmer had the ninth.

During another week in May I went 8 for 21 and got a lot of local press in Arkansas for hitting two home runs over the Deep-Dish Pizza sign. The papers were saying that I was hitting home runs as easily as dialing 1-800-DELIVER.

By June things kept getting better and better. In the first

week of that month, I was named Texas League Player of the Week. In eight games I went 14 for 34, a .412 clip, with five doubles, a triple, and eight RBI. I also stole four bases and had an on-base percentage of .444.

By mid-June, I had 16 stolen bases. In an organization without much speed, that put me at the top of the heap with the Rangers. By this point I began to wonder when my opportunity was going to come. I felt like I had taken all the lessons I had learned in the Florida State League, that I had shortened my swing, and that it was paying big results. I was working really hard with the batting coaches in the Rangers system, and the team was encouraging me to steal as much as possible.

At the same time, my body had developed into that of an athlete's—I had been eating well and lifting weights for nearly four years now, and it was showing. I was very happy where I was, and I know that the Rangers were happy, too.

Things were going along this way when we—the Tulsa Drillers—had a series against El Paso. At that time the El Paso team was affiliated with the Milwaukee Brewers. I had an excellent series. I stole the show. By this point I had played 66 games with Tulsa. I was batting .297 with 7 home runs and 31 RBI.

Meanwhile, back in Arlington, something was happening that would change my life. Pete Incaviglia, the Rangers power-hitting outfielder, hurt his neck, and the Rangers leadership—Tom Grieve, the GM, and Bobby Valentine, the manager—didn't have anyone to replace him when he went on the fifteen-day disabled list. They looked around their farm system for a player, and they saw me. Tommy Thompson, the manager of the Tulsa team, said these words to me: "You're going to the big leagues."

It was right before the game against El Paso, which I played in. I looked around in wonder and excitement, but I didn't say anything—at that moment. I waited until I went home to my apartment and found all my friends there. I said, "Hey, guys. I'm going to the big leagues!"

They thought it was a lie. Some of the guys said, "Well, you're going, but we'll see you back here in about fifteen days."

I said, "This is the only chance I'm going to need. You're not going to see me here again." I had made the Texas League all-star team, so I felt confident that I would be able to hold my own in the big leagues.

Then I made the call. It was late in San Pedro de Macorís, but this news couldn't wait. My heart raced as I heard my mother's voice. I was very emotional because this was a great day not only for me but also for my whole family.

We had made it.

Mireya Sosa:

Mikey said, "Mom, I'm going to be a big-league ballplayer." All he had ever done was work, he had always been so dedicated, and for a few years now people had been telling me, "Your son is excellent." And now here he was telling me things that made me cry.

He said, "Mom, I'm going to give you what my father couldn't."

All I could say was, "God bless you, son. God bless you, son."

Sammy:

The next day, as I was running out to catch a flight, I called Bill Chase and told him, too. I wanted to share the news with all the people who had known me when I was Mikey. Now the only thing left to do was to leave.

The Rangers had just finished up a homestand and were about to go on the road. They were going east, and there would be a day off before we'd start playing on a Friday. My first game would be a doubleheader, to make up for a game that had been rained out earlier in the season. The amazing thing was that I wasn't going to be making my major-league debut just anywhere. No, my first big-league game would be played at Yankee Stadium.

I got on a plane in Tulsa, made a connection through Dallas, and flew first class to the East Coast. I got to New York on a Thursday, a day off, and met up with my new teammates at the hotel. I couldn't believe that now they were *teammates*.

And I have to say right here that Julio Franco was the main person who helped me and took care of me when I was with the Rangers. Julio sometimes had a reputation for being a tough guy or being moody, but he wasn't that way with me. I lived in his house. He bought me a lot of nice things. He let me drive his cars. His mother was there, too, and she was very, very nice to me. Julio is an excellent person and someone whom I will never forget.

He even taught me some lessons. In the spring of 1989, the team was in Puerto Rico for an exhibition game, and I remember being with Juan Gonzalez. He was showing me around his town, and we were driving in a car together. Suddenly, we noticed that we were going to be late for the game. We were playing the White Sox, and I remember thinking that the Texas manager, Bobby Valentine, was going to kill us if we got there late.

I started telling Juan, "Man, we had better tell Bobby we got a flat tire or something." And we did. But Julio dressed us both down in front of Bobby. He knew what was going on and told us what our responsibilities to the team were. As I said, he was a great person to me.

We went to the ballpark together for that first big-league game. I'll never forget the incredible feeling the first time I walked onto the field at Yankee Stadium and saw the famous facade and all the history there. It was fantastic.

There I was, ready to play, and that's exactly what Bobby Valentine did—he played me. The team was very much considered a contender for the American League West title. Even though it was only June 16 and we weren't even at the halfway point of the season yet, there was a reason to feel optimistic in Texas.

We were just coming off a three-game sweep of the California Angels at home, part of a 7–3 homestand that sent the team to New York feeling good about things.

The sweep of the Angels had pulled us within a half game of them for third place. Overall, we were four-and-a-half games behind the then-mighty Oakland Athletics, who were formidable but missing some key players in mid-June.

Jose Canseco, the league MVP the year before, was sitting out the entire first half of the 1989 season with a broken bone in his hand. And Dennis Eckersley, the best reliever in baseball at that time, was sitting out the entire month of June on the disabled list. Now was the time to make a push, and we were excited that Bobby Witt and Kevin Brown would be pitching for us in the Bronx.

It was an overcast, muggy day at the stadium. The Yankees were having a bad season, the beginning of a franchise slump that lasted until the mid-1990s. That year they finished 74–87, and their manager, Dallas Green, was fired before the season's end.

Their problem was pitching. Andy Hawkins was their ace. He went 15–15 that year, with a 4.80 ERA. No other Yankee pitcher won more than seven games. Unfortunately for us,

Andy Hawkins was pitching that day. He was the first big-league pitcher I faced—and I faced him right away. I was leading off the game.

I wanted to be aggressive, and right away I got a pitch I liked and singled. I charged around first base and took my lead. Too bad for us nothing happened.

In the sixth inning, with Hawkins still pitching, I hit a double and felt elated as I rounded first and went to second. Our shortstop, Scott Fletcher, hit a line drive that the Yankee right fielder, Jesse Barfield, misplayed, and I scored—one of three unearned runs we got off Hawkins that day. But it wasn't enough. We lost, 8–3.

Then we lost the nightcap, 6–1, in a game that was delayed by more than two hours by two rain delays. Before the day was over, I had two hits and made an error, and we had lost twice. Welcome to the major leagues.

After New York it was on to another legendary baseball stadium, Fenway Park, in Boston. We lost the first game of that series. But in the second, I had a moment I will never forget. On Wednesday, June 21, I faced the great Roger Clemens. Right away, we fell behind 3–0, and things looked really bleak because Clemens looked unbeatable. He was throwing serious gas.

By the time I first saw him in June 1989, Roger already had two Cy Young Awards and had been an MVP. But Roger was 8–4 going into the game that evening and was struggling a bit on a team that would just finish above .500 for the year. Still, I have to say that I have never seen anyone throw harder than Roger Clemens. His fastball just exploded, and I remember before the game Ruben Sierra walked up to me and said, "Roger Clemens tonight, rookie. Get ready."

We managed to push a run across in the top of the fourth to cut Boston's lead to 3–1. Then I came up to bat in the fifth, my second turn at the plate. The next day, the *Boston Globe* described the moment this way: "Clemens struck out the first batter, then faced Sosa, whom he had blown away with a high fastball in the first inning. Sosa got one that was slightly more manageable this time, and he put it into the net."

Home run. My first big-league homer, and I hit it off of Roger Clemens! I remember running around the bases and watching the ball fly over the Green Monster in left. And my hit made a difference. It totally silenced a rabid crowd of 34,338. And it seemed to have an effect on Roger—or so the papers said. "Clemens never seemed to recover," wrote the *Dallas Morning News*.

He walked the next two batters, gave up a couple of hits, and we blew the game open. When it was over, we had won 10–3, and I had the memory of a lifetime. My first big-league home run came against a superstar who later went on to be selected to baseball's All-Century Team. When I see the videotape of that homer today, I marvel at how young I looked. Compared to today, I looked skinny. And once I had connected, I didn't do anything but run around the bases quickly. Years later, my home run trot would be a little different.

On this night, back in the Dominican, people were celebrating right along with me.

Omar Minaya:

That day I was flying to the Dominican Republic on business. Amado Dinzey picked me up at the airport, and I got to break the news to him that Sammy had hit his first big-league home run against Roger Clemens. We were both so excited and so happy. We really felt like he had been our signing and that we had had a hand in his success.

That night, after we finished working, we went out to celebrate. Presidente is the most popular beer in the Dominican, and I think that night we had a couple of Presidentes.

Sammy:

Four days later I had my biggest game yet as a professional—4 for 5.

Then in one game in early July against the Seattle Mariners, I got three hits, and for a time I kept right on hitting, continuing a fast start. But I came to learn that big-time pitchers make adjustments.

Soon I was seeing nothing but breaking balls, and my average started to plummet. At the same time, the team's hopes of staying in the hunt with Oakland were starting to fade. We were losing and the Athletics were winning. All the while, the Athletics were putting distance between themselves and everyone else in the AL West.

My frustrations were summarized in one game in Cleveland, in mid-July. We were locked in a tie in the eleventh inning. We had a runner on first, and it was my job to move him over with a bunt. But after two tries, I didn't do it. Luckily, we won the game anyway.

But I began to show my youth. When I look back now, I just wasn't ready for the big leagues. I didn't have the experience—either physically or mentally—to be there.

But I was getting experience in other ways that I hadn't counted on. As I said, we were locked in a fight in our division, trying to chase the powerhouse Athletics. Then, on June 21, the same day I hit my first big-league homer off Roger

Clemens, the Athletics got Rickey Henderson in a trade with the Yankees. That made them an even more powerful team. The papers in Dallas were making the comparisons: the Athletics get Rickey Henderson while the Rangers are bringing up Sosa.

It wasn't a criticism of me but of the Rangers, who were chided for not being able to pull off a deal like the Henderson trade. That was the difference between the Athletics and the Rangers, everyone said.

I began hearing that my name was being thrown around as part of a trade deal. In fact, two names kept coming up: mine and Harold Baines, the great outfielder for the Chicago White Sox.

In fact, I was getting a heavy dose of maturity all at once, because while all this was happening, I got told something I didn't want to hear: I was being sent back to the minor leagues.

I had lasted twenty-five games with the Rangers. My average had dropped from over .300 to .238. I hit one home run and had 3 RBI. I was not happy about being sent to Oklahoma City to play in triple A. And it showed. In ten games there, I batted only .103.

It was a humbling experience. I remember being really uncomfortable in Oklahoma City because I thought I could stay in the big leagues. One day I was at the triple-A park, coming out of the clubhouse and going to the hotel, when someone came up to me and said, "Sammy, I want to talk to you." I didn't know who this man was, so I ignored him and kept walking.

He called me again and I said, "Who are you?"

He said, "I'm Larry Himes." He then asked me why I hadn't run out a grounder in batting practice.

I said, "I didn't run because I'm upset about being here. I should be in the big leagues." Imagine that!

I had no idea who he was, but the next day I found out.

Larry Himes was the general manager of the Chicago White Sox, and, despite what he saw and heard, he had enough faith in my ability to trade for me and give up the most popular player on his team, Harold Baines.

It was a big trade and one that wasn't universally accepted in the White Sox clubhouse. In the papers, Larry Himes had to defend his reasons for making it. "It's an unpopular decision as far as the fans are concerned, but sometimes *unpopular* means exactly that—unpopular. It doesn't mean it's a bad decision."

The White Sox were looking for young, exciting talent to add to a nucleus of up-and-coming stars like Ozzie Guillen, Robin Ventura, and Frank Thomas. Along with me, the White Sox got Wilson Alvarez, who was only nineteen but was already showing great promise.

The Rangers got a professional hitter in Baines, a thirty-year-old veteran they hoped would drive in a lot of runs and complement their lineup.

Larry Himes:

When we were looking for who we could get for Baines, and we went through all the scouting reports, the first guy on our list was Juan Gonzalez. But Tom Grieve said, "We can't make a deal with Juan Gonzalez in it. He isn't going to be traded."

And I knew this was going to be the situation anyway. So I said, "Okay, fine. Is Sammy Sosa available?"

Grieve said, "Well, we hate to give him up but, yeah, we'll put him in there."

This went on over a two-week period, but before I made a deal I needed to see Sosa play. So I and two others from the

White Sox flew to Oklahoma City to watch him play. We were there for four days. And the most impressive thing I noticed was Sammy's enthusiasm and energy. It was really hot in Oklahoma City, but after batting practice, when all the other players had gone inside, Sammy would be out there alone, hitting a ball off a batting tee. He had a big can of balls next to him, and he'd just put a ball up on a tee and—whack. Then he'd put another ball up on a tee and—whack. I said, "Maybe he is just doing this today." But for four days it was the same thing. Those were things that I picked up on, along with his natural skills.

At that point we were asking ourselves, "What are we getting back for Harold Baines?" Harold Baines was a premier hitter, an all-star, our franchise player. But after seeing Sammy, we kind of settled on the idea that he would be like a Minnie Minoso–type guy. Minoso had been a great player for the White Sox in the 1950s, a player I really liked. So here I was looking at Sammy in that mold: a guy with a tremendous arm who could hit between 15 and 20 homers a year and steal 30 bases. In our scouting reports we gave Sammy's arm the top grade possible, and he had the ability to play great defense. With his speed we thought he could be a very exciting player.

We were building a young team and thought Sammy would fit really well with our club. When we looked at the difference between Juan and Sammy, it was like the difference between head and shoulders—Juan Gonzalez stood alone and then Sammy was on another tier. Sammy has gained about forty pounds since I first saw him, but at that time he wasn't projected to be a power hitter—he didn't have that type of body.

Juan was already a nicely framed big guy. He had a great swing, he was more disciplined and a more polished player. And he had a good arm, but Sammy could outrun him. I guess it was just easier to project on Juan at that time. The Sammy Sosa of today isn't the same Sammy Sosa I saw back then. He has grown into who he is. But don't get me wrong, I was very excited about getting Sammy. As a club, we didn't have any talent at all, but we were starting to put talent in place. I was looking for guys who could run and throw, and Sammy fit the mold. He was a guy that we needed.

Sammy:

Carlton Fisk, who was a leader on the White Sox then, said of Wilson and me, "Who are these guys?" He didn't find out at first because the White Sox sent me to their triple-A team in Vancouver right after the trade. I didn't play for about a week because at the time of the trade, I had slightly hurt my back. But soon I was back in the lineup, and I was aching to prove that I belonged in the big leagues.

In thirteen games in Vancouver I hit .367. During that stretch Larry Himes came down to see me and was convinced that I was ready. I got the call for the second time. I was going back to the big leagues.

Again, my team had a day off on the day I was called, and again we would be playing a road game—this time at the Metrodome in Minnesota. On August 22 I wore a White Sox jersey for the first time in front of 24,976 people in Minneapolis. Shane Rawley was pitching for the Twins, who were led by one of my favorite players, Kirby Puckett.

In my first time at bat, I walked. I did the same thing in my second turn.

But not on the third—I singled up the middle in the fifth inning. In the seventh, I grounded a single to left. And then, in the ninth inning, I hit my second career home run, a blast that landed six rows up in the left field seats at the Metrodome. We won the game, 10–2.

I went 3 for 3 with a two-run homer and a stolen base. After that, Carlton Fisk knew who I was.

"Nice debut, huh?" said my manager, Jeff Torborg. Unlike my first career home run, when the papers didn't quote me, this time reporters asked me what it was like to feel pressure. I would get asked this question again and again in later years. My answer on this night was basically the same as my answer today—except now I speak better English. I said, "Pressure? Pressure for what?"

I believed in myself. Some people mistook that for arrogance, but it's never been about arrogance. My faith in my abilities is just very strong. It's had to be. Now I was a member of the White Sox, and all I cared about was that I was in the big leagues and that I got to play.

Plus, I was in Chicago, an incredible city. My life was beginning anew. I was with a new organization, which was different from being in Texas, where everybody knew me. But I felt satisfied when I left Texas because I felt like I had set a good example for my hustle and my work ethic.

Melido Perez—a fellow Dominican—was on the team with me. I finished the last month of the season in Chicago and was playing well. I played thirty-three games with the White Sox down the stretch, and I batted .273 with three home runs. I had been traded, but I knew that was simply business. And when the season ended, I had accomplished the most important goal of my life. I was in the big leagues.

Now I prepared myself to fly home in style and to begin to truly help my family out of the poverty that was still a part of their lives. Even though I was in the big leagues now, I still wasn't making the kind of money that could change the lives of those in my family—not at that time. But I was getting closer.

I was a happy man when I touched down in Santo Domingo in October 1989. And my family was happy, too.

7

1990–1991: Swinging Wildly

When I went home after the 1989 season, the first thing I wanted to do was fulfill the promise I had made my mother: to buy her a house. But even though I had reached the big leagues, I wasn't yet making big-league money.

So, as I had done with many important decisions in my life, I sat down with Bill Chase to find the best way to make this dream a reality.

Bill Chase:

Sammy was making the major-league minimum in 1989 and had only played in the big leagues a short time, so he didn't have much money to buy the kind of house he wanted. So I said, "Well, business is good." I had three factories by then, and I remember saying something to my lawyer about Sammy's situation. My lawyer said that if I wanted, he would pay half and I could pay the other half—we would lend Sammy the money. All we had to do was work out a payment schedule, which we did. Sammy had found a house he wanted that cost something like fifty thousand dollars, so we made the deal. That was the first house he bought for his mother.

By then, I knew this kid was going to stay in the majors. I didn't mind helping him because one of the things I've always admired about Sammy is that he always paid me back. Like when I had to pay his income taxes the first time because he didn't have the money to do it—something like $12,200. He kept saying, "But I'm Dominican, I don't have to pay taxes in the United States." You live and you learn. But once the 1990 season got started, he repaid me.

Sammy:

Life was changing very rapidly. I was starting to make money for the first time and was able to spend it. I was starting to do okay financially, but I was still learning how to survive.

I had just turned twenty-one as I prepared for the 1990 season, my first full campaign in the big leagues. To think back on it now, I had gone so far, so fast. At thirteen, I wasn't even playing organized baseball. At fourteen, armed with my new blue glove, I took up the game seriously. By fifteen, I was being courted and then spurned by a number of big-league teams. At sixteen, I was negotiating my own professional contract—by myself. By age seventeen, I was sent to America without being able to speak a word of English. And just three years later I was in the big leagues. As a young man, it all seemed like an awful lot of time. But now I think back and am amazed at how quickly it all happened.

I was maturing but was still very young—I was still learning the game of baseball, still learning English and American customs. I was still trying to learn all the other important things about my profession: how to dress, how to act, what to say to the press, where to eat, how to order in restaurants, whom to trust, whom to distrust.

But while people like Bill Chase, Omar Minaya, and Larry Himes could help me, they couldn't live my life for me. There were some things I had to learn the hard way, on my own. And for me, before the season even started, I was already learning some very important things about life.

Bill Chase:

I remember that on opening day of the 1990 season, I was heading to the game with Sammy's brother Jose Antonio when he said: "Oh, Sammy has something to tell you." I asked what it was. And he said, "I think Sammy better tell you."

So after the game Jose Antonio said, "Sammy has something he wants to tell you."

So Sammy looked at me and said, "Oh, I'm married."

Married!

Sammy:

I was young and had made a mistake, but I wouldn't learn how big a mistake until later. Yes, very soon, I came to regret this decision and learn a lot about life in my new world.

But in the meantime I had the most important season in my life to prepare for. The White Sox were coming off a horrible year in 1989. The team had finished 69–92, in dead last place in the American League West. If it hadn't been for the Detroit Tigers, who lost 103 games in 1989—we would have had the worst record in the league.

As Larry Himes said, the team wasn't very good but we were striving to get better with the help of young players brought over in trades—like me—and home-grown talent from their minor-league system.

Showing up in Florida that February for spring training, we were a collection of kids, veterans, and journeymen. Larry Himes and Manager Jeff Torborg chose Ozzie Guillen and Carlton Fisk as our co-captains.

Ozzie, who is from Venezuela, was our shortstop and by then was one of the most popular players among our fans on the South Side of Chicago. Carlton Fisk, our catcher, had been playing in the big leagues since I was a small child back in San Pedro.

Along with me, there were a lot of new faces on the White Sox. In 1990 Robin Ventura was getting ready to play his first full year in the majors, just like me. He played third base, and that spring the papers were saying he'd be the first third base-man with star potential on the White Sox in a long time.

Scott Fletcher, who had come over with me from the Rangers, was our second baseman. Carlos Martinez, who at twenty-five was only in his second year, played first.

In the outfield I played right. Lance Johnson, who also played his first full season in 1990, played center. And Ivan Calderon, of Puerto Rico, played left.

We were still playing in old Comiskey Park, an ancient place that was built in another era, when outfields were huge. Luckily, Lance, Ivan, and I had what Larry Himes wanted: we were all really fast. Our pitchers would be thankful for that. The three of us ran down a lot of potential doubles and triples. Going into the year, our best pitcher was my countryman, Melido Perez. And that year there was another young White Sox prospect readying himself for his first full season in the big leagues, the right hander Jack Mc-Dowell.

Yet despite our enthusiasm, talent, and optimism, no one gave us much of a chance that year. On opening day, the *Chicago Tribune* wrote, "The White Sox will finish last again in 1990."

Larry Himes likes to say that young players "don't know that they're bad or what they're supposed to do—they just know how to play hard." And that's what we did. And damned if we didn't win, too.

While everyone was busy saying that we wouldn't be ready to compete until 1991, we proved everyone wrong. We started winning right away, though I personally got off to a slow start. For the first week I was batting about .200, until the Cleveland Indians came to town and I hit a pair of triples in a 9–4 win. But I didn't stop there. I also drew a walk and then showed my speed by going from first to third on a single.

A short time later, I hit a home run into the upper deck at Comiskey. Then, in a game against my old teammates, the Rangers, I hit a slow roller in the infield during a thirteen-inning marathon. I exploded out of the batter's box and ran so fast that my friend Julio Franco had to rush his throw, which went awry. I ran to second and scored the winning run on a single by Lance Johnson.

I was trying really hard, showing up at the ballpark early. On Easter Sunday, I was at the park at 8:00 A.M., doing extra hitting drills with our batting coach, Walt Hriniak, who played a big role in a critical phase in my career—critical, but unfortunately not positive. In fact, Hriniak is one of the few people I have negative things to say about in baseball. But we'll get to that later.

The bottom line is that 1990 was a joy ride for the White

Sox and me—an excellent season. We took everyone by surprise. The press was writing positive stories about me, putting to rest the criticism that surrounded the trade that had brought me to Chicago.

For the first time people were writing about my background and asking me questions about my youth in San Pedro. In one story a meeting I had with Walt Hriniak was recounted for everyone to hear. Walt was asking all of us hitters if we could truly say that we had worked hard. I answered honestly. "I've worked hard every day of my life." Our manager, Jeff Torborg, said hearing my words gave him "goose bumps" because he knew I was telling the truth.

Still, not everything was easy for me in 1990. By late May I was mired in a slump, at one point going 8 for 40 at the plate. Jeff Torborg gave me a couple of games off. He and Larry Himes knew that with all the young players we had on the White Sox, they had to be careful.

I was young and playing like it. In one game in late June against the California Angels, I got picked off first base, I dropped a ball in right field, and then I hit a home run to win the game.

Larry Himes:

You could see the talent in him. He was electrifying. Sammy would make diving catches for you in the gaps and in the alleys. He'd lay out flat in the air and then throw a bullet into the infield. But then again, he would bobble a ground ball he was about to throw home, or he'd catch the ball and throw it thirty feet up the line. There was no balance in his game. While acknowledging the fact that he would throw the ball off the screen or strike out swinging when the pitch was in the dirt, I would always say that you had to be patient with him.

I was kind of in a position of defending him when he did things that didn't fit the expectations of a major-league player. But the bottom line was that he did very well for us. He understood that he was the focus of the Baines trade, and he would do things that were just great. He had all the ingredients, and it was just a matter of time.

I mean, here was a guy that was really learning how to play baseball and doing it at the same time. He could have spent the whole year in triple-A, and I don't know if that would have been better for him. He probably would have had a tremendous season in Vancouver.

But we weren't in a position to do that. I needed to have someone to justify the trade that we had made. But when you think about it, he hadn't played that much triple-A ball by 1990—either before he came to us or after. This kid came from double-A to the majors and hadn't even spent a whole year in double-A. He just needed a little time to prove himself.

I think the way the industry looked at him then is that opposing managers knew how to get him out because his strike zone was so bad. Sammy had a strike zone then that was from the top of his hat to his shoe tops. You'd see him strike out on a curveball in the dirt. He'd get three and two with a man on, the pitch would be over his head, and he'd be swinging at it. Sometimes, he made it tough. But you never got down on him because of his energy or his enthusiasm or his work habits. They were always there. He just needed someone to help him and to guide him. But Sammy has had to learn a lot of things on his own, which is a shame.

Don't get me wrong, Sammy had a heck of a year in 1990. He hit 15 home runs, stole more than 30 bases, and had 70

RBI. Considering that he only hit .233, he stole a lot of bases and was very productive that year. And the fans loved the excitement that he brought to the field.

Sammy:

I was still one of the boys back in 1990. I had long, curly hair and a mustache. I was one of the kids in the clubhouse but I was proud of my season because, if I hadn't been a strong person, I would have never been in the big leagues in the first place.

Yes, I had made 13 errors that year, more than any other outfielder in the American League. But I was also the only American League player to reach double figures in home runs, doubles, triples, and steals—I had 15, 26, 10, and 32, respectively.

Off the field I was still paying off debts I owed and worrying about my family. On the field, the team enjoyed a 94-win season, enough in some years to win a pennant. But not when you're in the same division as the Oakland Athletics. The defending world champions, they won 103 games that year. And no wonder—their lineup was filled with superstars like Jose Canseco, Rickey Henderson, and a certain fellow named McGwire. But what did my mother always say? Life brings both good and bad—and sometimes at the same time. She was right.

While the White Sox were having their best season since 1983, Larry Himes—the GM who had filled the team with many of its stars—was fired in a dispute with the team owner. I felt bad because Larry had shown so much faith in me by trading for me. I didn't know it then, but that move would have serious implications for me.

I also learned much later that people who cared about me—who had known me from my first days as a pro—were worried that just such a thing would happen, that I would lose a valued mentor before I had become an established player.

Omar Minaya:

My only fear for Sammy at that time was that he would be in an organization where there wasn't someone looking out for him—that he would be in a situation where people would be forcing things on him. Sammy doesn't do well when you try to force anything on him.

Sammy:

Omar's words proved to be prophetic. And on top of that, I had a serious issue I had to contend with away from the field. By late 1990 I had gotten a divorce.

Bill Chase:

Sammy was a young man who didn't know any different. He met a girl, an American, he became infatuated with her, and they got married. But it was quickly clear that this was not going to work out. This was a brief episode in his life— from only January to August of 1990. But it resurfaced in February 1991.

Sammy:

I came to spring training in 1991 with high hopes. But my personal problems off the field involving my divorce the year before, coupled with bad press, led to the most difficult season of my career. It was nothing but problems and heartache through that whole wretched spring and summer. On top of that, my family suffered another tragedy with the death of my stepfather. In the end I batted a miserable .203. I hit only 10 home runs, had only 33 RBI, and stole only 13 bases.

The year started badly for me because the White Sox chose to platoon me with Cory Snyder in right field. I did not like that decision and said so. Still, I did have my up moments. On opening day, I hit two home runs against the Baltimore Orioles, one of them a three-run shot.

But things went so badly that year that by late April I had been dumped from the starting lineup. By then I was batting .071. I felt that my struggles at the plate started with Walt Hriniak, the batting coach whom I mentioned earlier. He wanted me to hit a certain way that wasn't my style. And I truly felt that changing my swing is what brought on all my problems and I believe hurt my career in my early years. Walt Hriniak and I were not a good match.

He would have me out taking batting practice at 6:00 A.M.—6:00 A.M.! And if I showed up at 6:01, he wouldn't want to work with me. But, as I said, it was the batting style that Hriniak wanted me to use that was my biggest problem. It was the style he wanted all players to use: head down, weight shifted back, swing down on the ball, drop your shoulder, and release your top hand from the bat on your follow-through.

Even worse was that after a while I was so crossed up and so tense that I actually had to look in the dugout after every swing. Can you imagine that? I'm a big-league hitter, and I

Hanging around the batting cage with Manny Alexander (*left*) and Jose Hernandez (*right*). Jose is a talented player from Puerto Rico who had started in the Rangers organization a year after me. Manny is from San Pedro like me and has been a great friend and teammate on the Cubs. COURTESY OF CHICAGO CUBS/ STEPHEN GREEN

Every time I hit a home run, I salute my mother with a touch to my heart and a blown kiss. COURTESY OF CHICAGO CUBS/ STEPHEN GREEN

During the home run race in 1998, the media turned up more and more as Mark McGwire and I approached the old Roger Maris record. COURTESY OF CHICAGO CUBS/ STEPHEN GREEN

My goal was to become one of the top players in the game—like San Francisco Giants outfielder Barry Bonds. COURTESY OF CHICAGO CUBS/ STEPHEN GREEN

Hitting home run number 61 to tie Roger Maris's old home run record on September 13, 1998. COURTESY OF CHICAGO CUBS/ STEPHEN GREEN

September 13, 1998, was a day I had dreamed of. After hitting home run number 61 in the fifth inning to pass Babe Ruth and tie the old Roger Maris record, I hit number 62 in the ninth inning and the Cubs won the game 11–10 over the Brewers. The crowd gave me an ovation that will remain in my heart forever. COURTESY OF CHICAGO CUBS/STEPHEN GREEN

I was excited about becoming the first Cub to reach the 30/30 mark, when I hit 33 home runs and stole 36 bases in 1993. COURTESY OF CHICAGO CUBS/ STEPHEN GREEN

The fans in Chicago are great: Sometimes they even use their bodies to spell out my name. COURTESY OF CHICAGO CUBS/ STEPHEN GREEN

As the home run race heated up at the end of the summer in 1998, there were press conferences before every game, with television, newspaper, and magazine reporters following us from city to city. I was on the cover of *Sports Illustrated* for the first time, and ESPN did a whole hour with me. COURTESY OF CHICAGO CUBS/STEPHEN GREEN

By August 19, 1998, Mark McGwire and I were tied at 47 home runs each—with six weeks to go in the season. The media attention was incredible, and what Mark and I were doing had people focusing on baseball again after all the negativity of the strike. COURTESY OF CHICAGO CUBS/STEPHEN GREEN

I've often been asked why I was so happy for Mark McGwire and why I kept calling him "the man." For me, it was just a way of showing my respect and admiration for him. Mark is a truly great player. COURTESY OF CHICAGO CUBS/ STEPHEN GREEN

I've been blessed with the opportunity to meet some of the greatest athletes of all time from all sports—including boxing legend Muhammad Ali. COURTESY OF CHICAGO CUBS/ STEPHEN GREEN

One of my favorite memories from the 1998 season: the night we beat the San Francisco Giants in a one-game playoff that put us in the postseason as the wild card team. COURTESY OF CHICAGO CUBS/STEPHEN GREEN

I'm proud to call Michael Jordan my friend. He won his sixth and final championship with the Bulls early in 1998. With the Cubs, we were just looking to improve as we started our '98 season. COURTESY OF CHICAGO CUBS/STEPHEN GREEN

I kept my concentration during the great home run race of 1998 by focusing on winning games rather than the media attention. COURTESY OF CHICAGO CUBS/STEPHEN GREEN

July 18, 1999, was Family Day at Wrigley Field. Back row, from left to right, my wife Sonia, my daughter Keysha, and myself. Front row, my daughter Kenia and my sons Sammy Jr. and Michael. COURTESY OF CHICAGO CUBS/STEPHEN GREEN

A favorite moment of mine from the 1998 season came on September 20th, when the Cubs held a Sammy Sosa Day celebration. Many of my friends and family were on the field with me. My mother, Mireya (*left*), was at my side for the very emotional day. COURTESY OF CHICAGO CUBS/STEPHEN GREEN had to look into the dugout for a coach's approval after every swing.

It wasn't long before my life was miserable. By the beginning of May, my batting average was still below .200. I couldn't believe the pressure I was under. It was terrible. I couldn't say anything because Hriniak was one of the key people who made the decisions on the team. They gave him a lot of authority. After a while, I felt I wanted to get traded. I didn't care.

In addition, there was a negative vibe in the clubhouse. At first I wanted to stay on the team so I did anything I could to stay. But I didn't understand how I could go from driving in 70 RBI and stealing 30 bases in 1990 to having so many problems with the team. Today, I'm still not sure how it happened. But I do believe it all began to change when Larry Himes left the White Sox.

Larry Himes:

There was more politics going on than talent evaluation. I hate to even blame Walt, because Walt is a hard-working guy. The problem was that the White Sox owner, Jerry Reinsdorf, gave more authority than he should have to Walt. Walt had a longer-term contract than the manager and the general manager. Walt was just this little bulldog who had all this authority wrapped up in him. It wasn't from me or Jeff Torborg—it was coming from the owner.

Walt was uncontrollable because of that power. He was trying to convert everybody to that hitting style, but Sammy was a natural swinger. Sammy needed to feel his way through the game, not through technical analysis. In the end, Sammy couldn't perform as they wanted him to, in this little box. In their minds that meant that the Sammy trade was a bad trade, so let's move him out. Sammy ended up getting caught in those things. They completely lost confidence in him.

Sammy:

On July 19 things went from bad to worse. The White Sox demoted me. I was going back to triple-A. But what made matters worse is that the demotion came at the same time my mother was making her first visit to the United States. I had arranged for her to get a six-month visa, and she and other members of my family were staying at my apartment. My brother Jose Antonio and my sisters had already come to visit—I always had family with me. But this was the first time Mama had made the trip.

I can't even begin to tell you how I felt when I got the news that I was being shipped out to Vancouver, especially when I had to tell my mother, who had come from so far, that I wasn't going to be there with her.

I came into my apartment, and there was my mother. She was sitting watching television when I told her. "Don't worry, Mom. This is the last time I'm ever being sent down. This is the last time anyone is ever going to use me like this." She just looked back at me. And then, as she has since I was a small child, she made me feel better.

Mireya Sosa:

My son always puts on a happy face, but I know when he's troubled. I didn't know that much about baseball, but I'm not dumb. I knew something was wrong. So when Mikey came up to me, I knew what he was going to tell me. He said, "Mama, they are sending me to triple-A."

And in a strong voice I said, "Don't worry, son. You go play like you know you can. You'll see when this season is over that you are going to be a different man. You're going to be stronger for this experience."

Sammy:

I packed my bags and flew to Vancouver. I was back in the minor leagues again after thinking I would always be a big leaguer. I was there for a month and played in 32 games. I hit .267 but toward the end of my stint, I was crushing the ball. It became pretty clear that the team would keep me in the bushes until September 1, when all teams could expand their rosters. I began to prepare myself mentally for playing the last month of the season and then seeing what happened after that.

Larry Himes:

When I heard they sent him to triple-A I said, "How could they send Sammy Sosa to Vancouver? How could they do this to this guy?" It offended me.

Sammy:

When remembering 1991, I can honestly say that it was the year I got the most experience. My mother had been right—

I was a different person, a stronger person. I even got called back to the team four days early, on August 28.

When I got back, the reporters asked me how I felt. I said, "This time I'll stay here forever. This time I'm a better man, and I'll do a better job."

And I even managed to have some bright moments down the stretch. In one extra-inning game against the Angels in late September, I was standing on second base with Lance Johnson up at the plate. He had the hit sign and swung away, chopping a high bouncer that he legged out for a single, allowing me to score from second. We won the game. I had that kind of speed and could still make exciting things happen on the field.

Then the season ended, thank God. I went home relieved, though hurting from my .203 average. I had never struggled so much on the baseball field. But I was still a big leaguer.

Oh, and remember those five girls who had once turned me down when I asked each if they would be my girlfriend, the ones who rejected me one by one? Little by little, they all came back, asking me to reconsider.

At that point I had money, and this time I was the one who said no.

Then that October I went to a nightclub called the Babylon in the Dominican. And from across the room, I saw a beautiful woman who just captivated me. Her name was Sonia, and she was the woman who truly captured my heart. I like to say that meeting Sonia was like the gift God sent to me. We got along right away. And we fell in love. She eventually became my wife, and we have a strong marriage to this day. And she has given me four beautiful children: Keysha, Kenia, Sammy Jr., and Michael.

The only thing I asked of her was that she love and respect me. After that I said I was going to make her a queen. In fact, meeting my wife was about the only positive thing that happened to me in 1991. Her love salvaged everything else.

But there was still a question hanging in the air as the year came to a close: What lay in my baseball future? In December, just before Christmas, stories began to run in Chicago, whispers that my days with the White Sox were numbered. First there was the story that the Sox were offering me to the Houston Astros for the pitcher Mark Portugal. There were also rumors that I would be traded to the New York Mets. My name was linked also to the Montreal Expos and the Cincinnati Reds.

Then, as a parting shot for the year, there was a story two days before Christmas that was very insulting. It read, "The question: What happened to a player once so full of promise?" The article was about me. An unnamed White Sox player said I was "uncoachable." The player was quoted as saying of me, "He's been brought up with 'I'm Sammy. I'll do what I want. I've been able to get away with hitting not-as-good pitching in the Dominican.'"

Yes, I was young and perhaps I did some things I shouldn't have done. I could be hard to be around. But every time I went to the ballpark, I gave it everything I had. I had shown I had promise and had even more potential. As 1991 gave way to 1992, I tried to learn from my experiences and show people what I could do. I learned that staying in the big leagues was harder than getting there. I thank God for sending my wife to me, particularly when he did. I needed all the support I could get back then. Now I had to put my baseball career back on track. It was my new goal to shoot for. But it took me a while to get my confidence back. It had been that bad a year.

8

1992:
Matters of Destiny

Larry Himes:

At this stage of his life, Sammy was a guy who was trying to make himself a big-league ballplayer. But he was very unsure of himself. And underneath the surface there was this thing where he had to prove himself. Even though he gave the appearance of being cocky and having everything under control, he really didn't.

Sammy:

Even before I showed up for spring training in 1992, the trade talk surrounding me was in full swing. And when I arrived in Florida, there was a new manager on the White Sox, Gene Lamont.

I had steeled myself to work very hard and fight through my problems with the team. But right away things just seemed to pick up from the previous year. In February Lamont was quoted in the paper as kind of warning me that I had better perform. "I told him he needs to play pretty good," Lamont told the *Chicago Tribune*. "We always talk about his potential and everything, but he needs to play like everybody says he can."

I tried to stay positive. Whenever asked, I told the press that I thought Lamont was a nice person.

And everyone kept asking me about Walt Hriniak. I said I didn't want a problem with anyone, that I just wanted to get along and do my job. I also said that I wanted to remain with the team. But it was no use.

I wasn't welcome in the clubhouse anymore. With Gene Lamont and the new general manager, Ron Schueler, I knew I didn't fit in anymore—I knew that just by the way people were treating me.

Then, on March 30, it happened. I had been traded again. They called me into Ron Schueler's office, and said they were dealing me. When the meeting was over, I stood up and said to both of them, "Thank you so much. You don't know how much I appreciate this." At that point they wanted to talk to me some more, but I didn't want any part of it. I said, "Thank you, thank you. You guys don't know what you are losing." They kept insisting that we talk some more, but I said, "No. No. No. There is nothing to talk about any more. Again I say thank you. Thank you." And then I left.

I went back into the clubhouse, and once I got inside, I took off my White Sox jersey and threw it straight in the air. I then told Ozzie Guillen and Ivan Calderon that I was leaving, that I had been traded.

I was so happy because at that moment, I felt like I had been through a war and I had survived. Or like I had been in jail and was being bailed out. It was like saying, "Free at last! Free at last!" So I packed up my stuff, and as I was going out the door, I said, in a loud voice, "Okay boys, I'm out of here. You guys will see me again! I'm going to be the best player in this game! You'll see!"

I had a plane to catch. At that moment I knew that this was one of the best things that could have happened in my baseball life. And I felt happy because here was my chance to overcome all the obstacles that had been in my way.

For the second time in a little over two years, I had been traded. And amazingly, the same man was behind both of my trades: Larry Himes. In November 1991 the Chicago Cubs hired Larry as their general manager. And when he made the deal for me four months later, it was his first trade as the new boss on the North Side of Chicago.

I was so happy that on that very day I was on a plane headed for Mesa, Arizona—the spring training home of the Cubs. When I got there, the first person I sought out was Larry. He was really happy to see me, and I was happy to see him. I gave him a hug and told him how much I appreciated his faith in me. I told him right then that I wouldn't let him down, that I would go all out in every game—I told him that he would never regret his decision.

As he had the first time, Larry had given up a lot to get me. Who did the Cubs trade for me? None other than George Bell, whom the Cubs had signed to a huge multimillion dollar contract in 1991 and who had been the MVP for the Toronto Blue Jays in 1987. As I've said before, George is from San Pedro de Macorís and was a legend in my town when I was growing up. Now all these years later, he and I had been swapped for each other.

Like the Harold Baines trade, this one generated a lot of publicity in Chicago. Everybody was asking Larry the same question: "Why did you do it?"

Larry Himes:

This trade was even more magnified than the last one because I was trading across town. Here I was coming from the
White Sox after having been the GM there for four years, and
now I was with the Cubs, and the first deal I made was with
my old team! The focus wasn't as much on Sammy as on me
because there I was trading George Bell, whom the Cubs had
gone out and gotten in a five-year free-agent deal. And at that
time George did a lot of things that Sammy couldn't do until
now. He had all the things Sammy needed to have: strike-
zone discipline and power. But he couldn't run. I was watching George play in spring training, and balls were falling in
front of him.

Now it was only spring training, but I look for guys to give
me effort, and I wasn't seeing that in George. That was
George as a player: great concentration and discipline with a
bat in his hand, but indifference to defense. And I was watching him and thinking, "We can't play like that."

Especially in the National League, you have to have guys
who can play both ends of the court. You can't just have a guy
who can carry a bat for you, as in the American League. The
White Sox wanted a number-four hitter, and I called and told
them that George would be available. And then we started
talking, and I said, "I want Sammy."

At that point I could have offered them anybody and they
would have given me Sammy. I wanted Sammy because I
knew he could play both ends of the court. I knew he was going to steal bases for me. I knew that he was going to cut
down fly balls in the gap. With him in the outfield, doubles
would become singles because of his arm and speed. In the
National League, you need people who can play defense in
the outfield.

What the deal came down to was that Jerry Reinsdorf

wanted money because George was making $3 million and Sammy wasn't making much more than the major-league minimum. I had to give them $400,000. That was critical to the deal—that's what Jerry was looking for.

The deal almost didn't come off because of a miscommunication, a freak accident, and dumb luck. The day the deal was going to be made, we had a spring-training game, and the White Sox sent someone out to watch George play. I told our manager, Jim Lefebvre, to play George only three innings because that's all they were going to watch. So three innings went by, and they said, "Okay, we can make the deal." Everything was fine, or so I thought. But for some reason, George went out and played the fourth inning. At one point, he was running hard trying to catch a fly ball, and he hurt his ankle. I was in my office when they ran in and told me, and I said, "Holy smokes. The deal is ruined!"

I thought he had broken his ankle. I was so angry I told Lefebvre, "I told you to take him out in the third inning! He wasn't even supposed to be in the game." I was so mad I had to go for a walk. I came back and brought George in to have our doctors look at him and get him an X ray. I was sitting there waiting, thinking, "God, I hope he's all right."

Meanwhile, the game was going on outside while I had my own game going on in my little trailer office. I was going nuts. This lasted about ninety minutes before the doctors came back and said the X rays were negative. It was only a twisted ankle. And thankfully George wasn't hurt. But he was angry with me when I told him he was being traded. Then I told him I had traded him for Sammy. And of course Sammy wasn't much at the time. So I was looking at George, and he was looking at me, and even though he didn't say it, his face expressed, "How in the hell could you trade me for . . . Sammy Sosa?"

Sammy:

When I look back on 1992—after having gone through the minor leagues and overcoming such a difficult barrier with the White Sox—I see that that was really the first year I began to have success. The kind of success where life was more full than before.

That Cubs team had some great players: Andre Dawson, Ryne Sandberg, Mike Morgan, and, of course, Greg Maddux. There were lots of really good ballplayers. Shawon Dunston was there, too. I had to make an adjustment. It was like moving into a house that wasn't mine.

I joined a team that had its own laws, but Larry Himes made changes that were favorable to me and, in the end, helped me a lot. Still, it was a change that was not popular with the fans in Chicago. They had traded George Bell. But some of the analysts who knew about baseball wrote that I had a good future. But when I got to the Cubs at the start of the season, the people did not accept me or receive me with enthusiasm because they didn't know me.

They didn't know the talent and potential I had. The Cubs started me in center field because in right field there was Andre Dawson, the leader of that team. Andre had been the MVP of the National League with the Cubs in 1987, a year in which he hit 49 home runs and drove in 137 runs. Andre had since put up two additional 100-RBI seasons and was a great and experienced ballplayer and a good person.

I was like a young boy, only twenty-three, and part of a trade where I was replacing a superstar. I knew I had to work hard to win over the fans. I played in center field because the regular center-fielder, Jerome Walton, started the season on the disabled list. The team had finished below .500 the year before and went though a managerial change during the season.

Because of that uncertainty on the team—a team with holes to fill because of injuries—and because no one yet knew what type of ballplayer I was, I was in for a lot of changes in just that one year. I played different outfield positions, and my spot in the batting order was all over the place. When Shawon Dunston got hurt, Jim Lefebvre even put me in the leadoff spot. At first, things went well. In my first five games, I went 7 for 22, scored five runs, hit three doubles, and swatted a home run.

By May 12 I was leading the team in runs scored with 20. I was hitting around .240 then—I would do much better—but that was still a big improvement over my days with the White Sox.

But my average began to suffer through the uncertainty of our lineup. When June 13 rolled around and 57 games had been played, I had been juggled around in five different spots in the batting order. Most of that time I hit leadoff or batted second because I was the fastest guy on the team and Lefebvre wanted speed at the top of his lineup.

People thought then that I might become a Rickey Henderson–type player—a blazing-fast leadoff guy who could hit homers once in a while. But as we all know now, that wasn't the type of ballplayer I was destined to be. No, my game wasn't the slap-hitting, just-get-on-base type of game required for a top-of-the-order player. I felt more comfortable down in the order, where I could swing away. But I didn't get down there too much early in the season. Mostly, I struggled in the two spot, where, in 23 games, I was 19 for 91. That's a .209 average. I just never felt comfortable high in the lineup.

Yet I understood what a tough time our team was having, so I did everything asked of me—I was a good soldier, though I was struggling. Then Lefebvre moved me down in the lineup. Right away, my average shot up to .280, and I began hitting home runs. In six games when I batted fifth or seventh, I was 8 for 22, a .364 average, with three home runs. In fact, in the four games I batted fifth, I hit safely in all four games. It was clear where I belonged in the lineup.

Overall, in the first 24 games of the season, I batted only .211 with 1 RBI, the one I recorded on opening day. I didn't drive in another run until May 5 and didn't get my first home run as a Cub until May 7. But down in the lineup, I took off and was feeling like I had always wanted to feel—like a productive big-league player.

On June 10, in St. Louis, I blasted two bombs in one game, the second time I had done that in my career. (The first time was against the Baltimore Orioles on opening day, 1991, when I was still wearing a White Sox uniform.) *Gracias a Dios!* Thank God!

But then, in my very next game, I faced another obstacle, another barrier, one I had never encountered before—injury. On June 12 Dennis Martinez of the Montreal Expos threw a pitch in tight on me. I tried to get out of the way, but it was too late—it slammed into my right hand with great force, breaking the fifth metacarpal bone. I went on the disabled list until July 27—almost six weeks. Thirty-four games with me on the sidelines. Just as I was hitting my stride, I was out. As my mother would say, it was destiny.

Larry Himes:

I was heartbroken when Sammy got hurt. And for myself, I said, "God, I don't need this." Sammy just didn't get a chance, and then I was getting beat up because on the other side of town, George Bell was spanking the hell out of the ball, driving in runs and having a hell of a year. So the trade looked like a bomb.

Sammy:

George had a good year that year, and so did the White Sox. They finished with an 86–76 record, while George hit .255 with 25 home runs and 112 RBI.

Meanwhile, I sat on the sidelines with my hand in a cast. The only thing I could do was keep working and not pay attention to things that could distract me. Part of that work took me back to Iowa, to the Cubs triple-A team, for rehabilitation. I couldn't seem to escape triple-A.

But this time it was different. I would never go back again. On July 27 I returned to the Cubs starting lineup. This is it, I thought to myself. This will be my time. It was a rare night game at Wrigley, a Monday night. We were playing the league-leading Pittsburgh Pirates, and there was a playoff atmosphere at the park. Just before my return, we had won five out of six games and suddenly found ourselves 6 1/2 games in back of the Bucs. They had lost five out of seven going into that Monday-night contest.

There were 34,990 fans at Wrigley. Greg Maddux was on the mound for us. The Pirates jumped out in front early. Then, on the first pitch I saw since going on the disabled list, I hit a home run to tie the game.

Later, the *Chicago Tribune* wrote that after my home run, "you could almost feel the Cubs believing they still have a shot to win this thing." Then the Pirates retook the lead. Then I singled to tie the game again. The Pirates loaded the bases with one out in the eighth. But Maddux recorded a strikeout, and then Jose Lind hit one to me in center, which I caught for the third out.

Then, in the bottom of the eighth, I hit a single. Lefebvre then called for a hit-and-run with Ryne Sandberg batting. It worked perfectly. Sandberg hit a single, and I flew to third base. Then Kal Daniels hit a fly ball to left—not deep, but deep enough to score me with my speed. We won the game.

I was back, and we were 5 1/2 games behind the Pirates with two months to go in the season. And we still had two games at home against the Pirates. We won the next day, and then, in the final game of the three-game set, magic struck again.

This time there were 36,554 people in the stands. This time the game went eleven innings. This time we spotted the Pirates four runs. And this time I came up to bat with one runner in the bottom of the eleventh.

Home run.

As I ran around the bases, I heard a sound I would hear a lot in the years to come: "Sam-my! Sam-my! Sam-my!" My teammates mobbed me at home plate. We had swept the Pirates, and I had played a key role in all three games. I went 7 for 15 in the series, with 2 home runs and 5 RBI.

The Cubs were now 3 1/2 behind the Pirates, and we could start to dream. We believed in ourselves, and I believed in myself.

Larry Himes:

Once Sammy got back from the disabled list, I could see him taking off. I said, "Okay, now he's got it made. Now we're going to see Sammy Sosa."

Sammy:

I was so full of confidence, I felt like I could do anything. Three days after sweeping the Pirates, we were in Shea Stadium playing the Mets, and I was standing on first base. The Mets' catcher, Mackey Sasser, called for a pitchout, but I stole the base anyway, and he threw the ball away. But instead of stopping at third base, I sailed around third and just kept running. I scored.

In nine games after coming off the disabled list, I went 15 for 39, a .385 average. I hit 3 home runs, scored 8 runs, and had 9 RBI.

Then, ten games into my return, destiny struck again. The Cubs were still in New York. I was batting against Wally Whitehurst in the first inning when I swung hard on a ball that caromed off my bat and shot straight down like a laser, smashing against my left ankle. Our trainer, John Fierro, called it "a one-in-a-million freak accident." It broke the large protruding bone in my ankle. John said he had never seen such a thing in seventeen years in baseball. The news got worse the next day: I was out for the season.

As a team, we got a lot of bad news down the stretch. We faded to fourth place and finished with a 78–84 record.

I finished the year playing in only sixty-seven games, with only 262 at-bats. I hit .260 overall, with 8 home runs, 25 RBI, and 15 stolen bases. But I didn't feel down. I had proved something to myself and had shown what I could do. I would try to come back even stronger the next year and finish what I had started in 1992. As for the rest, it was just a matter of destiny.

9

1993–1995:
Breaking Through

When 1993 rolled around, I still felt like I had to prove myself. I had come close in 1992, but fate kept getting in the way. In 1993 I wanted to let the Cubs organization know that I could be who I wanted to be. So I kept working. Jim Lefebvre was my manager, and he understood me, he knew the talent I had. He knew I could do well. That understanding made me feel like I had more freedom as a player, more opportunity to prove who I was.

Gone was the pressure I had felt with the White Sox. That whole system of having to look in the dugout after every swing for approval from Walt Hriniak had taken its toll. I remember when I first got to the North Side, I took my first swing in spring training and looked over into the Cubs dugout, like I was still programmed.

Later our hitting coach, Billy Williams, came up to me and said, "It's okay. Don't worry about that anymore." Now I had the freedom to do whatever I wanted at home plate. That lifted a lot of pressure off me. And the Cubs coaches went out of their way to make me feel comfortable.

I've always had the talent to play this game. But you can't

develop your talent if you are constantly under pressure and second-guessing yourself. That's what had happened to me. Little by little during that spring of 1993, my confidence began to go up. And I could tell that my teammates—people like Ryne Sandberg—had confidence in me.

I remember that the more time I spent with the Cubs, the more fascinated I was with Ryne Sandberg. In 1990 he had that beautiful year where he hit 40 home runs and drove in 100 runs. He had 100 RBI again in 1991. He hit 30 homers in 1989 and had back-to-back 26-homer seasons going into 1993. And he was a second baseman!

I had a total of 37 big-league home runs going into the 1993 season, a brief career that amounted to one full season, one year where I was sent to triple-A for six weeks, one injury-plagued season, and a cup of coffee at the tail end of 1989.

In my youth, I kept trying to figure out how Sandberg hit so many home runs. One day I spotted him sitting in the clubhouse, so I walked over and sat down next to him. And without him noticing, I was sitting there comparing my body to his.

And I told myself, "If this guy can hit 40 home runs, I should be able to hit 40 home runs because I'm a lot bigger than he is!"

But what Ryne had over me then was experience. And he had very quick hands. But here is one of the lessons I discovered about baseball: sometimes you can have talent, but you can't develop it until you find yourself. At the beginning of 1993, I was still finding myself.

Despite having my moments, 1992 was a hard year. And I was still trying to find my place on the team, to stay on the team. That was the most important thing.

I was still very young, only twenty-four. But that spring of 1993, I was already assessing the road I had taken to Mesa, Arizona, that February. I had already been traded twice; I know it was a part of the game, but some players get traded less than that in their entire careers. That spring I made a resolution to myself. It was time to finally find my place on a team, to find my place in baseball. And on one front I was already starting to reap the benefits of being a big-league player: During the off-season, my annual salary went up from $180,000 to $695,000 through arbitration.

On the field I was contending with the curious things that sports writers print sometimes. For example, when projecting my "potential" that spring, a writer compared me to the great Roberto Clemente. For those of you who don't know, Roberto Clemente was the greatest Latin player of all time—a superstar with the Pittsburgh Pirates from the 1950s to the early 1970s. He is idolized not only in his native Puerto Rico but also in my country and throughout all the Latin countries where baseball is played. When Clemente died tragically in a plane crash at the end of 1972, all of Latin America mourned.

Since then, a lot of Latin players have been compared to him, and writers have wondered who would be "the next" Clemente. Over the years Latin players such as Sierra, Gonzalez, Mondesi, and even me, have been compared to Clemente. And the list goes on and on. So when the question was raised to me in 1993—as it has been many times since then—I gave my standard answer: "I'm Sammy Sosa, not Clemente."

I've never been the kind of person to compare myself with anyone—I prefer to be judged on my own merits. Roberto Clemente is someone who was special and is special, particularly to those of us from Latin America. Clemente should be revered for his greatness both on and off the field. I honor him by wearing his number, 21. But in 1993 I was just trying to establish myself! Give me a break! I was just trying to make the team.

And on top of that, all of us in Mesa had plenty to contend with that February. The Cubs of 1993 were trying to build on our moments of success in 1992. But Andre Dawson had gone to the Boston Red Sox, and the organization tried to fill his departure by signing Willie Wilson. I worked with Willie that spring. I was looking for an experienced perspective to help me get better.

We got off to a good start as a team, and I came out playing the only way I knew how: full speed ahead. In one April game against the Phillies, I swung at the first eight pitches I saw: no taking pitches for me. Those hacks produced a two-run homer, a groundout, and a first-pitch single.

But as it would for the entire season, it was my base running that helped my team and began getting me noticed. In that Phillies game, we were leading 2–1 on my home run when I singled in the sixth inning, moving my teammate Derrick May from first to second.

Steve Buechele then grounded a slow roller to Mickey Morandini, then the Phillies' second and later my teammate in Chicago. I ran full out and saw Morandini field the ball, but instead of my conceding the out, I went for it. I did a head fake and sucked in my gut as I flew by Mickey, whose tag missed me as I danced along the edge of the infield grass and barreled into second base. Buechele was out at first, and the Phillies were screaming that I should have been out too, that I had run out of the baseline. Their manager, Jim Fregosi, their colorful first baseman, John Kruk, and Mickey were all screaming at second-base umpire Larry Vanover, who stuck to his guns. I was safe.

My countryman Jose Vizcaino, who was our shortstop that year, then hit a single, and soon we were up 4–1. We won the game. The reporters asked me about it later, and I said, "It was real close, but the ump saw the play." I didn't lie. The ump did see the play.

After a while, I started winning over the fans for the first time. As the Morandini play showed, I was an aggressive player then, just as I am now. What I was missing was the experience I have today. "He just needs discipline," is the way Lefebvre put it when asked about me in July of that year. "When he calms down and stays focused, you can see the improvement, but once he starts feeling good about himself, he loses that discipline." But there was no doubting my talent.

During the Fourth of July weekend, we pulled into Denver for three games against the Rockies. Going into a Friday night game, I had three consecutive hits and had been as hot as I had ever been in my career. Then, on that Friday night at Coors Field, I had a game I'll never forget.

I had six at-bats in an 11–8 win for us—six at-bats and six hits.

There were sixty-two thousand fans in the stadium that night, when my batting average jumped 19 points, from .265 to .284, in a single game. I became the first Cub since 1897 to get six hits in a nine-inning game. And suddenly I had nine hits in a row—one shy of the National League record.

The next day, with the record in reach, I came up to bat in the first inning with runners on first and second. I took the first two pitches for balls, then fouled off the next two. The Rockies' Curt Leskanic then threw a high fastball at me out of the strike zone—the kind of pitch I would have eagerly swung at when I was with the White Sox. Remember? Those were the days when Larry Himes said my strike zone was from the top of my cap to my shoelaces. But I laid off it. Full count. I then fouled off four tough pitches before Leskanic walked me. The walk filled the bases for Steve Buechele, who knocked a run home with a sacrifice fly.

In the third inning I flew out to Dante Bichette in right—my streak was over one hit shy of the record. But later the papers said I had shown a new maturity by getting a quality at-bat and getting a walk. And at the end of that Fourth of July weekend, I was named National League Player of the Week for the first time. I was growing. I was finally starting to do the things I had dreamed of doing.

In one tight game against the Dodgers at Wrigley in early August, we were trying to hold a lead when Brett Butler hit a shot into the gap in left-center. I was playing center field then, and if the ball got past me, the Dodgers would score at least two runs, and with Butler's speed in those days, they might have scored three, putting them right back in the game.

It was the type of fly that is so hard for an outfielder—the kind that sinks away from you at a high velocity. I ran as hard as I could, drew a line on it and went full extension, catching the ball just before it hit the ground.

After the game, which we won, they asked Lefebvre what he thought of my catch.

"Let's put it this way," he said. "I don't think I've seen a bigger catch. He just made the catch and turned the momentum to our side."

What made me happiest, as it always has in my incredible life, was being able to share my success with others. And in Chicago, during that summer of 1993, nobody was happier for me than Larry Himes.

Larry Himes:

To me Sammy's career took off in 1993. That was the most satisfaction I had. That's when I would say, "Man, he's got it. This guy's got the stuff." The only other guy I ever saw with that type of persona, with that type of confidence, was Pete Rose. I played with Pete Rose in the minor leagues, and Pete was the most confident player I had ever been around in my life.

Before 1993 Sammy didn't have confidence. But after 1993 it didn't make a difference if he would go 0 for 4. The next day he would be out there trying to beat you. So because of that, I derived the most satisfaction out of 1993. It proved that this guy was who I thought he was.

Sammy:

By this point I began to enjoy life a little more. I began to enter the realm of big-league players, and to distinguish myself among the truly good players in the league. By mid-August 1993, I had 27 home runs and was closing in on 30 stolen bases. Jim Lefebvre had worked really hard with me and had stuck with me. When asked about my progress and success late in the 1993 season, Lefebvre said, "When [Sammy] first came up, he made it on pure, raw talent, and he got labeled. This is one of those things you see in baseball. We label guys real quick. 'This guy's undisciplined. He doesn't think up there. He's overaggressive'—all those type things."

By the time September rolled around, I had a lot of desire to keep playing my game—that's how I made my reputation. I was still young, and I would still make mistakes, but the future was looking bright.

On September 2, I hit my thirtieth home run of the season, against the New York Mets. And then, on September 15, at Candlestick Park in San Francisco, I stole base number 30, becoming the first Cub player to achieve the "30/30" mark, which had only been attained by a small handful of players. In fact, I was only the tenth player in National League history to go 30/30 in a season. I remember looking into the dugout as my teammates stood and applauded me. It was a great feeling.

When the game was over, I took that "stolen" second base back to Chicago, and I still have it, here in my home in Santo Domingo. It symbolized sacrifice and faith and a new beginning for me.

When the season was over, I had 33 home runs, 36 stolen bases, and 93 RBI. I had batted .261 in 598 at-bats, the most at-bats I had had in any season since I started playing professional baseball. Of course, I wanted my average to be higher. But considering from where I had come, .261 meant nearly a sixty-point improvement from the horrible season of 1991.

But the 30/30 mark was what I was proudest of because it put me in a select group of players. Who else had gone 30/30 in a season?

Henry Aaron, Willie Mays, Bobby Bonds, and his son Barry, who won the National League MVP award that year.

By the end of the season, I knew I was finally being accepted as a total ballplayer. Getting on the plane to fly home from my best season ever, I was taken by surprise—a beautiful surprise—when my whole town was waiting for me upon my arrival.

A caravan of people greeted me. It was an incredible thing. At that moment I knew I had attained a different level of success and that my life was changing. There were all these parties thrown for me, lots of people came to see me. It was really beautiful.

I bought another home for my mother. I started to reap the benefits of my success. My contract came up, and I signed a one-year deal with the Cubs worth $2.95 million.

At that point, things got easier for me in every way. I bought a beautiful house for myself—a home in one of the most gracious neighborhoods of Santo Domingo.

I lived there until early in the year 2000, when I moved into an even nicer home. But at that point in my life, my new house was a blessing—a home I could not only share with my beautiful wife but also with my mother and all my brothers and sisters.

I would make sure that they were all well cared for. We had all come so far from where we had started. I was filled with satisfaction for what we had achieved. But I was also filled with motivation—I knew I could play even better. After the 1993 season and before the 1994 campaign, the Cubs invited me to an event for fans in Chicago that kicked off the coming season. I went.

Larry Himes:

I remember being at the party, eating a hot dog, when Sammy came in. He was all flashy. He had all his flashy clothes, not like the conservative suits he wears today—he was stylin'. So he saw me from across the room and came over. And he had this huge gold piece hanging around his neck. I mean it was *huge*. And on it was the inscription, "30/30." I said, "Sammy, what the hell is that?" He just smiled and said, "This is 30/30, man." There were some people who thought that was dumb, but I thought, "He's got to have the most nerve of anybody I've ever seen. I mean, he's got guts to wear that. But I'm thinking to myself that there was no way this guy was going to let himself be embarrassed." What greater motivator is there? By wearing that, I thought, he's going to go out there and try to do even better.

Sammy:

Larry was right. After 1993 the only thing I wanted was to go out and do even better.

1994

Going into the 1994 season, my career was being described in glowing terms again, as it had before the 1991 season knocked me off track for a while. Jerome Holtzman, the dean of Chicago baseball writers, wrote in early 1994, "At 25, [Sosa's] a developing superstar. In time, if Sosa continues to improve, [the trade that brought him to the Cubs] could be among the best deals in Cubs history, a reverse of the 1963 Lou Brock trade."

Everybody in Chicago knows that in 1963 the Cubs traded away Lou Brock, a speedy outfielder, to the St. Louis Cardinals for next to nothing. What followed for the Cubs were years of mediocrity while Brock led the Cardinals to two world championships in the 1960s and became the all-time stolen-base leader until his record was broken years later. Today, Brock is in the Hall of Fame. Now my name was being compared to his.

It's amazing what one good year will do for a career. I was very proud of what I had accomplished and tried to explain to people how I was feeling. The gold necklace I bought was an example of that pride because the 30/30 symbolized not only what I had done in a season but also what I had done just to get there.

I told Jerome Holtzman, "I wanted everyone to see the necklace. I'm the first one to [reach 30/30] from the Dominican. I feel happy to wear it. It reminds me of what I did." Some people misinterpreted the necklace as a sign of arrogance, but it wasn't about that at all—I was just really proud of how far I'd come in life.

After having played most of 1993 in center, I took my place as the Cubs' right fielder in 1994. Right field was the position where I felt the most comfortable. But while I was settling in, the team was having a tough time. Tom Trebelhorn was our new manager. And he had a rough beginning in his new job.

We got off to a terrible start—0–8 at home, 3–10 overall. Soon Larry Himes and the coaches were holding meetings trying to figure out what to do. All of us were frustrated— there is nothing worse than losing.

By early May, we had lost our twelfth consecutive game at home and felt so bad that we gathered as a team after the game. At that point, we were 6–18. Twelve straight losses added up to the longest losing streak in Wrigley Field history and the longest by any Cub team in 117 years.

The team was trying anything to reverse its fortunes. The lineup was completely shuffled and, at one point, I was put in the leadoff position. It produced the same results as it had in 1992—I just wasn't meant to be a leadoff hitter.

Things just went from bad to worse. Our clubhouse was described as "poisonous" in the press. For my part, by late June, I was on pace to go 30/30 again. And if my career were an education, with each year teaching me something differ- ent, then 1994 was the year I learned about what happens to a team when things go very badly.

For the season I led the Cubs in every key offensive cate- gory. But at the same time, a reputation was growing around me in the frustration of that year that would take me a couple of seasons to dispel. The word from "anonymous" teammates in the press was that I was a "selfish" player. The rap started that year. They said I'd steal bases in lopsided games or do anything to pad my statistics.

I said then and I say today that I am not a selfish player. All I ever wanted to do was win, to do my job, to help my team. I'm not above saying that I made mistakes in my younger days. But I was not a selfish player. After spending so much time on the disabled list in 1992, I played the 1993 and 1994 seasons straight through. I didn't feign injuries. I didn't make excuses. When it was game time, I was ready.

Shortly after the "selfish player" label surfaced, my manager addressed it. "It's that syndrome of trying a little too hard. You can fault the results, of course, because we have the results. But you can't fault his effort."

I decided that I would let my play on the field do the talking. And I knew that Wrigley Field hadn't cornered the market on trouble in baseball. Storm clouds were gathering all over the league as the players prepared for a possible strike in August. By late July, I was hitting close to .300 and had 24 home runs and 61 RBI. In a full season that would put me on pace to hit 40 home runs and steal 31 bases—that would have given me back-to-back 30/30 seasons.

Only Willie Mays and Ron Gant had ever done that in National League history. But we were losing, the club was unhappy, and I was open to criticism. I just refused to get caught up in it.

It was also a tough time for Larry Himes, who had always been so good to me.

Larry Himes:

After a while, I stayed away from Sammy in the clubhouse because some of the other players were jealous of him. And it was the most petty jealousy that I had ever seen. Here you've got a new guy coming into the clubhouse who is a young guy, who has never really played in the big leagues much. And you've got veteran players jealous of the young guy?

Sammy:

Amid our struggle in Chicago, the strike hit baseball on August 12, canceling the season after 113 games. We finished dead last in the National League Central with a record of 49–64.

I finished the year batting .300, with 25 home runs and 70 RBI in a season cut short by 49 games. I also stole 22 bases. When I went home early that year to the Dominican, I had been through a lot in 1994. I was far more experienced in life than when I had left.

1995

When the strike ended and cleared the way for the 1995 season, there was some question as to whether I would leave the Cubs. One newspaper even wrote that I was going to the Boston Red Sox.

Yes, I did talk to the Red Sox about the possibility of playing there, but it proved to be a blind alley—the result of all the confusion following the baseball strike. It gets technical, but the bottom line was this: during negotiations between players and owners, there was a chance that I might be considered a free agent. But when the players and owners came to agreement, I wasn't—based on how many years I had played.

It's not worth getting into the details because the bottom line was that I was still a Cub and happy about it and would be eligible for free agency in 1996. When asked what I thought about my talks with the Red Sox, I said what I felt: "It was nice to feel wanted, but now I want to stay here."

Judging by the whole issue, I was entering a different category of players by the time 1995 rolled around. In two seasons—including the shortened year of 1994—I had 58 home runs, 58 stolen bases, and 163 RBI in 1,024 at-bats.

But also going into 1995, Larry Himes—who had been so good to me through the years—was gone. His job became the victim of our horrible year in 1994. Based on how badly things had gone for me with the White Sox when Larry had left, people wondered how I would do this time. The *Chicago Tribune* wrote, "[This] raises the question of how the talented but sometimes unbridled Sosa will cope with a new regime." I felt bad for Larry, but make no mistake: I was going to prove who I was in 1995.

And, thankfully, the Cubs as a team got off to a much different start than we had the year before. We won our first three games in a row, with me putting an exclamation point on our home opener by hitting a bomb that propelled us to a 4–3 win over the Montreal Expos. The papers said it was one of the longest home runs in recent memory—measured at 442 feet—though a lot of people thought it went a lot farther.

We had a new manager in Jim Riggleman that year, and suddenly our clubhouse was optimistic again. And I got off to the best start of my career up to that point. By May 22 I was batting .337. The best part was that I was adjusting at the plate, making slight changes in my approach that brought great results. In one game in an early Dodgers series, their reliever Felix Rodriguez struck me out in a pressure situation. The next day I faced him again. I came up in the bottom of the thirteenth inning of a game that had gone on for almost four hours. We were losing 1-0. There was a man on, and Rodriguez was trying to get me out again. This time I parked one into the center-field seats. And what made me proudest of all was that my home run sealed the nine thousandth win in Cubs history. I went 3 for 5 that day and 8 for 13 in the series, with two home runs.

And I was reaching out to the fans, and they were responding. By this point I was acknowledging the fans in the right-field stands whenever I ran out there. People said I had a swagger, that I strutted around. But I was just being me. And I wanted the Cubs fans to know that I cared about them, that I heard them, and that they meant a lot to me.

It's always been that way between me and the fans at Wrigley—they love to watch me play, and I love to play for them.

The fans I have always cared the most about are the kids, the children who come to the games with their parents and look up to the players. By 1995 I had two small daughters of my own, and I remembered how I felt when I used to see George Bell or Julio Franco around San Pedro when they were big leaguers and I was just a kid.

So I always went out of my way to wave to the kids, to sign their autographs, to talk to them. My mother always used to say that it didn't cost anything to open your heart to people, to show them you cared. I had so much, I just wanted to give back. And by the time we were reaching the halfway mark of the season, people were mentioning my name in a way they never had before—as a candidate for the All-Star Game.

One game from the first half of the season stands out in my mind. On July 1, before 39,652 fans at Wrigley—the biggest crowd of the year to that point—we were locked in a back-and-forth game with our rivals, the St. Louis Cardinals. After our promising start, we had gone 9–20 in June and were trying to turn things around. But we gave up four runs in the top of the seventh and fell behind, 7–6. I had hit a three-run homer earlier in the game to put us ahead, but now we had to rally, which we did.

Remember Rey Sanchez, my old Sarasota Rangers teammate? He was now a Cub. In fact, he was already in the organization when I first arrived in Chicago in 1992. Anyway, Rey led off the seventh with a walk. Mark Grace then hit a single, and I came up with Rey in scoring position. I got a low, outside pitch and drove it to right for a single, scoring Rey for the tying run. It was my fourth RBI of the game.

I then stole second and scored on Luis Gonzalez's single.

We won the game, and a huge crowd went home happy, as did I.

Then the wonderful news came. I had been named to the All-Star squad for the first time. Felipe Alou, my countryman and manager of the Expos, had picked me as a reserve. It meant so much to be included with the best players in the game. And it was so gratifying that all the work I had done and the obstacles I had overcome were paying off.

As the game approached, I led the National League in RBI and was hitting .289 with 15 home runs. America hadn't gotten to know me yet—I finished only sixteenth in fan balloting—but I felt confident that if I kept playing my game, the accolades would come.

The game was in Arlington, Texas, where I got my start as a big-league ballplayer. It was a thrill to be among all those great players in Arlington. I had a great time. And I entered the game in the sixth inning and got to bat in the ninth. I flied out to left, but I didn't care. I was honored to be there. And I'll tell you this. Once you play in an All-Star Game, you want to go back again. That was my new goal.

And so was making the playoffs. We had a legitimate shot at a wild-card spot that year, and we were doing everything we could to win. But we got off to a bad start in the second half, losing eight of nine games at one point. Then, on a charter flight I tried to loosen things up by joking with my teammates on the plane. Some of my comments were taken the wrong way, and I apologized later.

I was just trying to loosen people up. In the Dominican sometimes when things are going bad, we try to look at the bright side of things, to laugh about things. But Jim Riggleman talked to me about it and said, given our losses, that my timing was bad.

I guess I was still learning. But I was taking all these lessons to heart. As the trading deadline approached on July 31, there were even rumors that I would be sent to the Baltimore Orioles.

By this point, I was the highest paid player on the team, making $4.3 million. Ed Lynch was the general manager, and he denied that he was talking seriously with the Orioles. What did I do? I just kept playing. I've known for some time that there are two things in baseball: what happens on the field and business off the field. By late July, I had proved my commitment by playing in my one hundred and sixteenth consecutive game. In August the *Chicago Tribune* wrote, "As Sammy goes, so go the Cubs."

What they were referring to was my season so far. In the first thirty-three games of the year, when I hit .326 with 10 homers, the Cubs were 21–12. In the next sixty-four, when I slumped to .240 with nine homers, we were 28–36. I was twenty-six and suddenly had a lot more responsibility than I had ever had in baseball.

People were looking to me for the first time. And so, with everything I had, I worked to move my game to the next level. In mid-August I went on a 6-for–15 tear, and we started winning again. I kept hitting as August went on, batting .349 over a twelve-game stretch, which included more big moments for me in Denver.

In three consecutive games I hit three-run home runs— one for 433 feet, another that traveled 435 feet, and the longest shot, 458 feet. By August 20 I was second in the National League in RBI. When reporters asked me what it was like to play at Coors Field, I said, "This is a good park to hit in."

Suddenly, we were back in the wild-card race—2 1/2 games behind the Houston Astros. I then had a two-homer game as we pounded Florida 10–2. On August 24 I hit my seventh homer in seven games: seven in 22 at-bats. Four were three-run homers. My streak surpassed one posted by

Ryne Sandberg in 1990, when he hit seven home runs in nine games.

Then the powerful Atlanta Braves pulled into Wrigley for a crucial four-game series. Our playoff chances hung in the balance and, as they did to so many teams, the Braves dominated, winning the first three games. I got one hit in 10 at-bats, striking out six times. Things looked bad for us, but I refused to let down.

In the fourth game, I hit two home runs and we won, 7–5, salvaging a game and staying in the hunt. The home runs were numbers 28 and 29 of the season. And I reached a career-high 95 RBI. Of my performance the *Chicago Tribune* wrote, "Sosa also may have silenced some of his critics who contend that the bulk of his homers come in games when the Cubs are far ahead or behind."

Then, in early September, we got a rematch against the Braves, this time in Atlanta. Forty-nine thousand fans jammed into Fulton County Stadium and watched as I hit two home runs and drove in four runs in a 6–4 Cubs victory. It was our fifth win in six games, and for the first time in my career, I passed the 100-RBI mark. Also for the first time my name was mentioned as a possible MVP candidate.

But unfortunately, we didn't make the playoffs. We battled and fought and hung onto our dream until the next-to-last day of the season, when we lost a heartbreaker to Houston, 9–8, at Wrigley.

In the ninth inning of that game, I hit a shot to the warning track that would have won it for us, but it was not to be. Still, we held our heads high as a team because no one expected us to contend.

It was the best year of my career. I played in all 144 games of the season, leading the league in games played. (Editor's note: the 1995 season started three weeks late, hence a complete season was 144 games.) I was a 30/30 man for the second time. I batted .268 with 36 home runs and 119 RBI. Twice in August, I was voted National League Player of the Week, the first time a Cub player had done that twice in a season. After the year I won the Silver Slugger Award and was named to the *Sporting News* All-Star Team.

I was very proud when I went home that year. I had broken through and now had my sights set on another goal: becoming one of the truly elite players in the game.

10

1996–1997:
On the Verge

There was some question as to whether I would return to the Cubs after the 1995 season. But I wanted to come back, and I did.

In January 1996 I signed a three-year, $16-million deal that boosted my yearly salary to about $5.3 million. I wanted more years on the contract, but since the strike teams have been stricter on approving multiyear deals. So the Cubs and I compromised: I would take fewer years than I wanted, but in return would be allowed to test the free agent market after the 1997 season. The team had signed Mark Grace to a similar deal. Anyway, we got it done, and I got to stay at Wrigley.

It's still incredible to think about it all. Among my friends and my family everything was the same—we shared our lives as we always had. To this day my brothers and sisters often live with me. My mother comes over frequently and stays over. Every Christmas and New Year's we spend at her house—all of us together, as we always have.

Don't get me wrong, I'm not going to pretend that I don't enjoy the benefits of being a big-league ballplayer. That would be a lie. But the essence of my life—the people I spend it with, the friends I have, my time with my family— have pretty much remained the same since I was boy. Except now we eat a lot better.

By spring 1996 my family was commuting back and forth regularly with me to the States. All the loneliness and solitude of those early years were a thing of the past. And I had gotten my first taste of being the team leader, of knowing that my team's fortunes depended a great deal on me.

I was eager to bust out because if I did, I knew the Cubs would have a better chance of winning. And make no mistake, winning is what I want more than anything. Those were the feelings that were in my heart, though I would learn that I still had a little way to go before that message had gotten across to everybody.

After struggling a bit in the first two weeks, I got things on track in a way people love and remember—by hitting really long home runs. One game against the Cincinnati Reds stands out. It was April 17, a chilly day in Chicago, as it often is in the spring. Only 13,023 fans were in attendance, but they were treated to a ten-inning game that we won, 8–6, when I launched a bomb toward Waveland Avenue.

The *Tribune* wrote, "[Sosa hit] a tenth-inning shot that didn't start its descent until local air traffic control gave it clearance. . . ." That day, I hit my third and fourth home runs of the season and drove in four runs.

I did struggle early that year, though. By early May my average was down around .200. Maybe I was trying too hard. But those things happen in baseball, and experience taught me to keep pushing. Then on May 5 at Wrigley, I just started swinging naturally, and the results were a 450-foot home run onto Waveland to win the game in the bottom of the ninth. The papers said that I jumped around the bases like a little kid at Christmas, and I did—I've never been ashamed of showing my emotions. I love the game. I had gotten into it as a way of helping my mother, but along the way it got to me—it got under my skin, and I don't mind showing my love for it.

I was happy because we won and happy because I had been mired in a deep slump. I went 0 for 18 at one point. Every day I worked with Billy Williams, our batting coach then. I reviewed tapes, I took extra work in the batting cages, I hit off the tee, and I analyzed my batting stance and my pitch selection.

All ballplayers know what I'm talking about because all ballplayers go through slumps. The key to being a professional is to stay positive, to not get down on yourself. I've always been able to do that, thanks to Mama. Thanks to God, the home runs started to come in bunches by mid-May. I had 15 by May 24. I also had 35 RBI, 35 runs scored, and 100 total bases—totals that put me among the league leaders in every category.

Remember when I was so skinny as a kid, as a prospect, and as a rookie? With each year I had worked on my body. I lifted weights, I took care of myself, and I worked out really hard. And with each year, I developed physically more and more. Using the work ethic my mother taught me, I would train all winter long, particularly working on my arms and chest. As I said earlier, I can often be found in my home gym lifting weights and working out at 1:00 A.M.

As it had in 1995, that work was paying off in a big way in 1996. And by the middle of June, I was getting noticed around the league. "Sammy Sosa is a five-point player right now," said Tommy Lasorda, the manager of the Los Angeles Dodgers, around that time. "Do you know how many five-point players are in the major leagues? Not many. A five-point player has to hit with power, hit for average, have outstanding speed, have an outstanding arm, and be very good defensively."

I was still working on the part about hitting for average, though I was making real progress. As I said earlier, Billy Williams and I were working very hard together. When referring to my average, which was .256 lifetime at that point, Billy said, "Sammy is getting there. He's learning how to hit the pitch on the outside to right-center. That right there can give him 30 points." The outside right-center of the plate. Remember that. It will be an important point later.

Anyway, by June 20 I was leading the National League in home runs with 23 and was one of the league leaders in RBI with 53. People were starting to project that over a full season I would hit 52 and drive in 119 RBI.

I knew I could because throughout my career I had always hit best in July, August, and September. In June, Tony Muser, a coach on the Cubs, was asked about me. He said, "Sammy is so intense and aggressive once the game begins, who's batting behind him is not a factor. I've seen him for four years, and I'm convinced he's out to prove he has a chance to be the best ballplayer who has ever lived."

He was right. And everything was going great for me by midseason 1996. I was still leading the league in home runs and was among the league leaders in RBI. At the beginning of July I was kicking off what ended up as the best month of my career up to that point. By the time July was through, I was named National League Player of the Month, the first time I had ever won that honor.

That month I hit .358 in 26 games, with 22 runs scored, 10 homers, and 29 RBI. From June 11 through July 18, I would put together three 10-game hitting streaks. In other words, in that five-week period I hit in every game I played but the ones on June 21 and July 4.

Hitting fifty home runs seemed a very realistic goal. Yet somehow, some way, I got left off the All-Star team. When the word came down, I couldn't believe it. I didn't scream or toss things around the clubhouse. When reporters came and asked me about it, I didn't raise my voice. But was I disappointed? Yes, very much so.

Bobby Cox, the manager of the Atlanta Braves, made the decision. Still, what I always said was that I considered myself an all-star even if Cox didn't pick me to the team. I was an all-star in my own eyes. And I think my play demonstrated that he made a mistake. I was playing well. I had the numbers of an all-star. But he didn't pick me. Even if the fans didn't choose me, I had earned a spot as a reserve. I think that might have been the first time the player leading the league in home runs didn't get selected to the team. And if I wasn't the first, I'm sure I was on a short list of home-run leaders who got snubbed.

So yes, I felt hurt because I felt I deserved to be on the team. There had always been lots of obstacles for me in my life, lots of complications. I've always overcome those obstacles, once my disappointment had subsided, I just looked upon the All-Star snub as another obstacle to overcome.

Filled with that motivation, I had my best week of the season soon after the All-Star Game. Between July 22 and July 28 I hit .400 (12 for 30), with four doubles, four home runs, nine runs scored, and 10 RBI. I was again named National League Player of the Week.

Unfortunately, the team wasn't doing nearly as well. In mid-July, when I passed the 30-home-run mark for the third time—not done by a Cubs player since the 1960s and the days of Ernie Banks and Ron Santo—I could have cared less. I wasn't happy. We were losing. So when people talked about me being on pace to challenge the great Hack Wilson's Cubs record of 56 homers in a season, it meant nothing to me.

Thank God for the fans at Wrigley. They kept supporting

us, and they kept supporting me. It was in 1996 that my friends in the bleachers began bowing to me after I hit a home run or made a great play. Still, as I said earlier, I was going through a process in these years.

Jim Riggleman hadn't been with us long as a manager, and he spoke to the criticisms that I was pushing aside, but hadn't completely disappeared. "[Sosa] never hits the cutoff man, they'd tell me, and he runs too reckless on the bases," Riggleman said. "Well, I've never seen any of that. Sure, he makes mistakes. But there seems to be blanket criticism of him. I can't understand why. . . . People are starting to ask me why he's not considered in the same category as Barry Bonds and Ken Griffey. I think he's getting there. I think his time has come. He's one of the elite."

Though I was criticized in print during these years, those who levied the criticisms never did so by name. It always seemed to be "anonymous" critics. That's okay. I'm not an envious person, and I don't hold anger in my heart. I just play.

And in 1996, that's what I did. And I was proud of the way I played. By July 19 I had played in 274 consecutive games. Meanwhile, in Chicago, my name kept getting linked to Hack Wilson's. People kept asking me if I could break his Cubs single-season home run record of 56, which he had set in 1930. And I kept telling people the same thing: "I never saw Hack Wilson play, so how can I make a comment about him?"

Still, his name kept coming up, particularly when I hit the 40-home-run mark with more than six weeks to go in the season. I felt more confident than ever when on August 20 we got set to play the Florida Marlins at Wrigley. Over sixty-two games going into that day, I was hitting .310 with 20 home runs and 54 RBI. When I raced out to right field, I was playing in my 304th consecutive game. And right away, things were looking up for us again.

I came up with the bases loaded, facing Mark Hutton. Digging in, I had to bail out fast because Hutton threw one in on me very tight. It hit me on the right hand. I took my place at first base and stayed in the game. But my hand kept swelling up until it forced me to sit down in the fifth. At first, all of us thought it was a deep bruise, but the pain kept getting more intense.

I barely slept that night because it hurt so much, but I had every intention of playing the next day until our trainer, John Fierro, told me the bad news: X rays showed that Hutton's pitch had broken the pisiform bone in my hand. I would need surgery to repair the damage. With six weeks and 38 games to go in the season, my year was over.

I finished with a .273 batting average, 40 home runs, and 100 RBI. Lots of people wondered what those numbers could have been had I played the full season. Maybe 50 or 55 home runs? We'll never know. Even though I was deeply disappointed, I tried to look on the bright side and to be there for my teammates.

Most of all, it hurt me not to be able to play for them. I took my responsibilities on the team very seriously. And for a player, nothing is worse than not being able to play—not to be there for your teammates. It's a terrible feeling.

A few weeks after my injury Jim Riggleman said, "We have been playing about .500 baseball this season. And the only reason we have hung in there with a chance to play .500 baseball is because Sammy carried us in April and May. That's why we are respectable."

The Cubs finished in fourth place in the National League Central with a record of 76–86. Meanwhile, I began rehabilitating my injured hand. I didn't let the lost opportunities of 1996 get me down. I knew I was close to my goal of being one of the game's elite players—I just had to keep pushing. I knew it was just a matter of time.

1997

Today people always talk to me about 1998, about the fantastic things that happened to me that year. It was a magical season, not only for me but for Chicago and all of baseball. But in my heart, I know that the groundwork for 1998, the foundation for all those great memories, were laid the year before. Before I had an army of media following my every move, before my friend Mark McGwire really even knew who I was, my life as a player was at a crossroad.

Before 1997 was over, I would experience anxious moments, reevaluate who I was as a player, and come to know things about myself that I hadn't known before. I would live through a season of negativity on a struggling team and face negativity as an individual player. Don't get me wrong—some great things happened in 1997, some beyond my wildest dreams. But aside from my beloved fans at Wrigley—and my family, of course—my story played out far from the glare of the national spotlight. That's why a lot of my fans and people in and out of baseball were surprised when I burst onto the scene in 1998. When I did, it's as if everyone asked, "Where did Sammy Sosa come from?"

In 1997 I was searching for answers to my own questions. These were questions that went straight to the essence of my baseball career, my approach to the game. All the little questions led to one big one: Who was Sammy Sosa as a player? Finding the answer required trust and faith—in myself and in others. That was not an easy time.

The year started not with talk of baseball but with talk of money and salaries. Everyone knew that I could test the free agent market if I wanted after the 1997 season, per the terms of my contract. That reality was hanging in the air when, across town, the Chicago White Sox signed Albert Belle to a five-year, $50-million contract soon after the 1996 season.

Then, in the spring of 1997, the Florida Marlins signed Gary Sheffield to a six-year, $61-million contract. Gary and I are almost exactly the same age—he's six days younger than I am. We both broke into the big leagues around the same time. And in 1996, he had a big year: 42 home runs and 120 RBI.

Because I had hit 40 home runs in an injury-shortened season, people began speculating about the kind of contract I could sign. But to be truthful, I was setting my sights lower. In fact, that spring I would have agreed to a $36-million contract over four years. But nothing happened because the Cubs wanted to wait until the season was under way before settling my contract situation.

Then, before the start of the season, a reporter asked me what I would do in 1997 given that I was on pace to hit more than 50 home runs until I got injured in August of 1996. Could I hit 50 in 1997? "Why not 60?" I answered. Then I got ready to play.

Going into that season, I had experienced losing. I knew what it was to be on a team that struggled. But nothing prepared my teammates or me for the first few weeks of the 1997 season. There is no other way to put it but this: 0–14. We set a new National League record for consecutive losses at the start of a season. Our play was like the April Chicago was experiencing that year—bitterly cold. The fans brought "lift the curse" signs to the stadium. We had team meetings—lots of them. It was terrible.

For myself, I was off to a slow start, and—as is my nature—I was looking for positives anyway I could find them. One day, the Cubs told me about a program in East Moline, Illinois, where thirty-nine kids and their mentors really wanted to come to a Cubs game but couldn't afford it. It turns out this was to be the first major-league ball game for these kids, young people being taught self-esteem and the importance of an education.

Once I heard about them, I was happy to invite them to a game as my guests. As I've said before, I love kids. It makes me happy to see them at the ballpark. It wasn't much when you consider what it was for and how much it meant to the kids. Sometimes I have to take a step back and put my life in perspective. It wasn't that long ago that I was shining shoes and struggling to find my way just like those kids. How could I forget the kindness of Bill Chase when I was a kid just struggling to get by day to day? He bought me my first glove. Treating these kids to their first game was just a small gesture.

Besides, it was one little bit of positive action at a time when things weren't very positive for us at Wrigley. Through April and into May, we were losing and losing and people kept asking me the same questions over and over: "When are you going to sign your contract, Sammy?" "Shouldn't you get paid the same as Sheffield and some of the elite players?" "Are you getting angry at the Cubs for not making a deal yet?" The truth is, I didn't want to talk about any of that stuff. I wanted to win, and I wanted to play the way I knew I could, and neither of those things was happening. Meanwhile, the papers began printing a lot of stories about whether the Cubs would or wouldn't sign me. There was even speculation that the Cubs would let me go. All I could do was keep playing.

And finally, in mid-May, I broke out of my slump. In six games, from May 11 to May 18, I hit .348, with four home runs, two triples, and 12 RBI. In one of those games against the San Diego Padres, I went 4 for 4 with 6 RBI— a career high for me up to that point. On May 18 I hit a key home run off Shawn Estes, who won 19 games that year for the San Francisco Giants. Then, for the fifth time in my career, I was named National League Player of the Week. On May 26, in Pittsburgh, I hit my first career inside-the-park home run. And going into June, I was still hitting well.

As the month went on, the questions about my future in Chicago intensified. Then came June 27.

The Cubs made a contract offer, and I accepted.

I became the third highest-paid player in baseball at that point—behind only Barry Bonds and Albert Belle. My agent, Adam Katz, had negotiated a four-year, $42.5-million contract that came with a $4-million bonus.

It's funny—in the spring I had asked for $36 million, and they decided to wait. Then I signed for $42 million. Later, I came to find out that the team's president, Andy McPhail, had asked some members of the team whether they should sign me to that contract, and some said no, that I wasn't worth the money.

I think there were some people on the team who didn't want the Cubs to sign me, but Mr. McPhail didn't pay any attention to them—he told me that he wanted to build the team around me. I felt very fortunate that the Cubs leadership had that kind of faith in me.

But the doubts about whether I deserved the contract weren't confined to certain members of my organization. There were many written reports that criticized the deal, that said I wasn't worth it. The biggest criticism was that while I was putting up big numbers, my team was floundering. One *Chicago Tribune* story said, "Some Cubs fans complain Sosa doesn't hit well enough when it really matters. Sosa was hitting .209 with men in scoring position. . . ."

I set out to prove that I did deserve the contract. I was playing in every game—I wouldn't miss a single one. I was averaging one home run every 17.8 at-bats, which put me among the league leaders.

Before the year was out, I hit my two hundredth career home run, at the age of twenty-eight. But things were still negative. We were losing, on our way to a 94-loss season and the worst record in the National League, a distinction we shared with the Philadelphia Phillies. It was a bad time, one where our losses and my strikeouts were getting more attention than anything else was.

Amid all of this, the Cubs tried to find any answers they could. One was to hire a new batting coach and take the unusual step of bringing him on during the middle of the season. His name was Jeff Pentland and had come to us from the New York Mets. He had also coached with the Florida Marlins, where Gary Sheffield had been one of his prized pupils. He had also worked with Barry Bonds. I didn't really know Jeff. But I had worked with a lot of batting coaches already in my career, and a lot of managers, too.

As Larry Himes said, a lot of the things I knew about hitting I had picked up on my own, and I had stuck to an aggressive approach, one that had gotten me to the big leagues, gotten me big numbers, and had made me rich. But at that point in the season, none of that mattered.

Inside of me, I hungered for more. Even though I had been so poor as a child and was now so rich, I couldn't be satisfied—or comfortable. There was a fire inside me to be the best, to excel every time I played. The reason I played in every game, why I didn't want to sit, was that when game time came around, no one was more excited than I was.

As bad as things were in 1997 for the team, I still couldn't wait to get to the park every day and play. It's just that there was a level of frustration attached to our every move as a team that year. And despite my increasing home-run totals and stolen bases, there was an increasing level of negativity toward me. I was experimenting with different batting stances and approaches at the plate that year while the new hitting coach and I slowly got to know each other.

Jeff Pentland:

I really began to notice that Sammy was a lot more talented than I had first noticed when I was in Florida. And as a coach I got pretty excited about that. But it was a miserable season, and we really didn't have much of an attack at all—I think we averaged nine hits a game and one run, unless Sammy hit a home run.

We didn't have a lot of power. Sammy had power, and when you played against him—as my teams did—you always had a feeling that if you threw the ball in his hot areas he would create some havoc. But he had a lot of holes in his swing. You could get him to chase balls if you elevated your pitches. His discipline at the plate was not what it should have been.

So when you looked at him as an outsider, you recognized the fact that he had some power and you recognized that when he hit the ball, nobody hit it as hard as he did. But you just felt like he was out of control all the time. The great hitters can repeat their swing consistently, and they seem to recognize and read balls better than the average player. Sammy wasn't doing that consistently at that time.

When I got to Chicago in 1997, I really didn't do anything with Sammy right off. At that point I wasn't in any hurry. I think what I tried to do was to get a good read on what he was doing and get a good understanding of where he could go.

What I realized when I started to break him down was that this guy could be something special. The two things that really stood out were his attitude and his aggressiveness. He is about as aggressive a person as I've ever been around. I've always felt as a coach that the more aggressive the player is, the better, because it's your job as a teacher to harness that aggression to where it's productive. At that point Sammy was aggressive, but he was wildly aggressive.

And there was no direction or control of that aggression. His holes in his swing were off the plate—you could get him to chase balls. And I don't think his recognition skills were really honed at that time. In other words, he was lacking in his ability to read pitches, which I think is critical. Obviously, the guys who do it best are the best hitters in our game: Barry Bonds, Gary Sheffield, and Jeff Bagwell. Those guys have tremendous ability to identify pitches when they are batting.

So early on I just tried to establish a trust with Sammy, which was not easy. That's because he had been through so many hitting coaches in his career. I didn't blame him for being a bit leery of me. Plus, I don't have a big-league background as player, so it was going to take some time. But I was there every day, and I showed tenacity in wanting to be his hitting coach. I wanted to establish a rapport with him. So I maintained a stubborn attitude and was around him all the time.

The thing I noticed about Sammy was that he was very, very emotional. And the thing that I tried to do was to understand what made him tick, to understand the man himself because he was going through a rough time. The club was terrible. Some of his teammates were talking about him. There was a period when he was having some problems with the manager and management in general. He had just gotten this huge contract. So what we ended up with was a guy who was very unhappy, even though he was one of the richest players in baseball.

Obviously, we were losing, and you're always going to blame the guy who makes the most money. And certainly, the people who weren't making as much money as Sammy were eyeballing him. And because of all this, Sammy was unhappy in 1997, and he really didn't have any reason to be. But I think the expectations of him were wearing him down a bit. The result was that, to a degree, he tried to be Sammy Sosa by himself.

But I don't think his personality would allow that. And when you try to be something that you're not, it makes you unhappy. He couldn't live that way. He needed the respect of his teammates, he needed the respect of the press and, most of all, he needed the respect of his country.

Sammy:

It was hard. I've never been on a team that was so pessimistic. For my part, my numbers were off from the year before. By mid-September, I had 33 home runs. The year before, I had 40 by August 20. When people asked me what I thought about my year, I told the truth: "I could have done better."

Then, in the last weekend of the season in St. Louis, our horrible season came to a negative close. I was trying to steal a base, and Jim Riggleman didn't want me to. It wasn't a personal problem, it was a problem between a player and a manager. Those things happen sometimes. But the problem was, he dressed me down in front of the other players. I told him that if he had a problem with me, to talk to me alone and not in front of the other players.

I'm somebody who respected Jim Riggleman very much. I mean, I make mistakes like any human being, but when that happens, you should just take a person aside and tell him— not do that in front of the whole team. What he told me was that I was a selfish player, that I only thought of myself.

I said, "No. I've never done that. And if you're going to question me that way, question the others as well. I played in all 162 games that year. I played hard. I never once showed up at the ballpark and said that I was hurting or that I was injured." I was always there, always ready.

It was a tough confrontation, and because it was in front of my teammates, it embarrassed me deeply.

Then the season was over. Toward the end I had a conversation with Jeff. He was trying to get me to change my approach to hitting. And before I went home to the Dominican, he prepared some tapes for me to study of other players and their swings. He wanted to begin working on them next spring. I went home that October with a lot to think about.

Jeff Pentland:

I didn't really get established as the hitting coach until toward the end of the season. It was then that I kind of approached Sammy and said, "Sammy, your numbers are good, but when are you going to be ready to play in the higher echelon of the game?" I really tried to challenge him.

I don't think he knew any different but to swing for the fences. The important thing about hitting is that it's like opening up a flower. When it's there and the petals are all folded in, you don't know how beautiful it might be. What I made Sammy aware of was that there was a lot of finesse and softness in hitting.

Up to that point Sammy's play had made him a lot of money. But I got the feeling that Sammy wanted more than that. So I tried to sell him on a different approach, to teach him to go against his instincts, to teach him that he didn't have to kill the ball to hit it out of the ballpark. We agreed that when spring training rolled around, we would start working together.

11

1998

Here's the funny thing about 1998, the year everyone still talks about. In spring training of that year, when Jeff Pentland and I would meet daily to discuss hitting, we set out many goals because we thought it could be a special season.

So we talked a lot about me taking more walks. We talked about me hitting the ball to the opposite field. We talked about hitting over .300. We talked about scoring over 100 runs. We talked technique. We talked game strategies and identifying pitches. We talked about my footwork, where I held the bat, how I held the bat, how I swung the bat. We talked all about hitting.

But going into that season, Jeff and I never—ever—talked about home runs. My fans might not believe that now—129 home runs and two seasons later—but it's the truth. Home runs were the farthest thing from my mind. Don't misunderstand: it's always the goal of a power hitter to hit with power. But I had a lot more important things to worry about than whether I would hit a lot of home runs, the most important of which was learning from my struggles from the year before.

To look at it on paper, I had put up solid numbers in 1997:

36 home runs, 119 RBI, 22 stolen bases. And there were other things that gave the illusion of total happiness in my life. I had the contract I always wanted, making me one of the best-paid professional athletes in the world. Considering my background and how poor my family had been when I was a child, my life story was already a rags-to-riches success story. And I suppose the story could have ended there—happily.

Believe me, I thank God every day for all that I have and I feel an obligation to give back to my people—to all people—who have cheered me and supported me.

There is no way to describe the feeling of knowing that I would never have to worry about my mother's financial well-being again. She could rest at last and enjoy her life, surrounded by her children and grandchildren. That gave me great satisfaction.

So did knowing that all of my brothers and sisters—Luis, Sonia, Juan Eduardo, Raquel, and Jose Antonio—had secure futures without the burden of poverty.

In Chicago the fans loved me, and I loved them. Who could ask for anything more?

I guess I could. What I still wanted, what drove me to work harder than I ever had before, was to be a star without any caveats attached to my name. I knew they were still there: Sammy Sosa hit 36 home runs, but he struck out 174 times, more than anyone else in the National League. Sammy Sosa drove in 119 RBI, but he hit .246 with men in scoring position and .159 when pitchers got two strikes on him. Sammy Sosa stole a lot of bases, but he did so in meaningless games and situations. He had a low on-base percentage and made reckless defensive mistakes.

I accepted all these criticisms as part of the game. I could look at myself in the mirror because I knew that when the bell rang, I always answered it. No one could ever say that I didn't try hard enough or didn't care enough. I cared deeply—about the fans, my teammates, the Cubs, about every game and at-bat, and about my reputation. But when I showed up in Mesa, Arizona, that February, all the old caveats were still around.

Right off the bat reporters asked me about 1997. I told them that I thought I'd had a "bad year," that I expected more of myself, and that I would dedicate the coming year to realizing my goals.

It's never bothered me to talk this way, to occasionally face up to my own shortcomings. There is no shame in it. We're all human beings, created equally. If you make a mistake, you should say so.

By the spring of 1998, I was twenty-nine, a major-league veteran. My career had already given me many valuable experiences. First, I had been a kid, a nobody, in this game. Then I was a highly touted prospect, an exciting rookie. Then, almost overnight, I was a clubhouse outcast and disappointment to the White Sox. I was the guy the Cubs were "foolish enough" to take in exchange for the great George Bell. I was a budding power hitter struggling unsuccessfully as a leadoff hitter. Then, when I began to find my groove, I spent most of that first Cubs season on the disabled list while George Bell and the White Sox piled up big numbers across town.

But then I became the tenth player in National League history to hit 30 home runs and steal 30 bases in a season—and then I did it again. And I would have done it again had it not been for the strike of 1994.

I had my best season in 1995, the year after the strike, when baseball fans were still angry and attendance was down. I was headed for a breakthrough year and 50 home runs in 1996 when I got injured again, stopping my season at 40 home runs with six weeks to go. It seemed like the breakthrough was finally within my reach.

Late in 1997, after Jim Riggleman confronted me in St. Louis in front of my teammates, the Cubs called a team meeting to discuss it and my role as leader of the club. Riggleman was there. So was Ed Lynch—the Cubs general manager—and Jeff Pentland. And me, of course.

We sat down, and they started telling me they wanted me to steal more bases, to drive in more runs, to get more walks, to strike out less. I sat there and listened. Listened hard. But then, during the meeting, Jeff spoke up and said, "Wait, Sammy Sosa isn't the problem here. He drives in 100 RBI a year." Jeff defended me, and I appreciated that.

We were building a relationship that spring of 1998, and he was encouraging me to try a different approach at the plate— to go against instincts that had gotten me where I was. If I were to put my finger on any one thing that turned the tide for me in 1998, it was those conversations that Jeff and I had in Arizona.

Jeff Pentland:

When I began to break down Sammy's approach to hitting, I noticed that he held the bat way above his head with the bat kind of hooked toward the pitcher. When he held the bat that way, it felt very strong in his hands, and what I recognized right away was how strong Sammy was. As a coach you try to establish a guy's pluses and minuses, and in Sammy's case his strength was a plus. But his strength was also hurting him.

I began explaining to Sammy that the strength in his setup and batting stance weren't important, that the only place strength played a role was at the point of contact and beyond. So he needed to be loose and relaxed at the plate to prevent his muscles from becoming too tight. I suggested that he lower his arms, and I used examples of great hitters in the big leagues. The strongest guy I ever played with was Reggie Jackson. He held his arms low to take the tension out of his arms and hands and to allow him to use his strength when it was important. Sammy's swing at this point was what we call a maximum-effort swing—he swung too hard. I mean, he's a tremendous athlete. So just by lowering his arms, the relaxation and looseness clicked in.

Then we started working on his footwork in the batter's box. Right now, the style of hitting that is in vogue is what I call a "tap step." That means that when the hitter is in the batter's box, he will move his front leg toward his back leg as the pitch is on its way. Then he will kind of tap it in the dirt and then step forward with his front leg as he swings. It's a way to shift your weight to your back leg, which is critical.

In 1997 Sammy was using a variation of that, and I asked him about it. I watched him use it, and to me he was doing it wrong. As a power hitter, all your power is in your legs. It's not in your hands and feet. And Sammy's movement was late and then too quick. Ideally, when your front foot touches back, the ball should be halfway to the plate. Sammy's feet were so late that when his front foot finally touched, the ball was in the dirt area of the plate. What that does is create a rush, and it makes the hitter have a sense of urgency, to swing too quickly. But what I've learned over the years is that you want to give the hitter as much time as possible to read and recognize the pitch. So I came up with a drill in spring training where Sammy would take his stance and then begin his movement. He would tap his leg back and then wait. Then I would throw him the ball, and he would step forward and hit it. We put a pause in there. Instead of having his feet go back and forth real quick, we changed it. It was, *tap back, pause, tap forward.* And he picked it up immediately because he is so talented.

Then we began working on it with a pitcher on the mound. What we came up with was that when the pitcher brought his hands down during his windup, Sammy would tap back. Sammy had to train his eye, develop a timing device. What came out of the tap step was that Sammy would begin to use his legs better than anybody in the big leagues.

Sammy is not a very tall man—I think around five feet, eleven inches—but he generates so much torque out of his lower body. Sammy was learning that power was actually more coordination and timing than brute strength.

What we were working toward was to make Sammy's aggression into "controlled" aggression. The other thing was to turn negative emotions into positive ones. He had to turn around some of the negative feelings he had toward some of his teammates and the press and understand that doing so was the responsibility of a superstar. He had to rise above that part of the game and rise above all the trite little things that were being said in the clubhouse because all that stuff is really meaningless.

Sammy:

That spring of 1998 was a very sad time for all Chicago. Our community lost one of our favorites—my beloved friend Harry Caray. Harry helped me so much. He was such a good person to me.

One time we were joking around and I said, "Harry, you've always been so good to me."

And he said, "Sammy, I only hang out with the stars. And you're a star."

He was just one of those special people, and I know he is with God now. We all mourned his loss. And so before the start of the 1998 season, I decided I would dedicate it to him. Every time I hit a homer, I would be hitting it for Harry—and for Mama, of course.

Remember when I said I could trace the great things of 1998 to the lessons I learned in 1997? It was in 1997 that I started blowing kisses to my mother after my home runs. Now I would salute Harry as well.

I've been fortunate to be around some of the great personalities in Chicago sports. Harry was one. Ryne Sandberg was another. Ryne was a terrific player, a player with class who always did what he had to do on the field and did it well. He was very steady, very calm. I really liked playing with him. I have played with Mark Grace for a while. He is a good player, a smooth hitter. I can only say good things about him.

And by the time I was getting ready to embark on the 1998 season, another Chicago guy familiar with making history was calling it a career. His name is Michael Jordan. Michael is the best, and I'm proud to say he's my friend.

I had a great spring training in 1998. I was feeling good, I was hitting well, and I was very optimistic. I felt like Jeff understood me. He knew when to push and when to back off—I thought he was a great instructor. Our team was picked by many to finish third in our division.

We had some new faces on the team. My countryman Henry Rodriguez came over to us from the Montreal Expos after putting up two solid years and a 103-RBI season in 1996, a year he also hit 36 home runs. They hoped that Henry would provide some protection for me in the lineup. Henry would play left field, Lance Johnson would play center, and I would play right.

Grace would be at first. We brought in Mickey Morandini to play second and take the place of Ryne Sandberg, who retired for good after the 1997 season. We would use a variety of players at shortstop. One was Jeff Blauser, and the other two were players whom I admire and like very much. One was Jose Hernandez, a talented player from Puerto Rico who had started in the Rangers organization a year after me.

The other was my friend and countryman, Manny Alexander. Manny is a San Pedro guy just like me. He had played with the Baltimore Orioles and New York Mets before he came to us in a trade in the latter part of the 1997 season. I can say right now, without hesitation, that Manny is the best teammate I've had in baseball. We talk all the time, and we've done a lot of things together. And he's always been very supportive of me.

Our pitching staff looked stronger at the beginning of 1998 also. We had Kevin Tapani, Steve Trachsel, and an amazing young prospect named Kerry Wood. And we had added Rod Beck in the bullpen. Despite the preceding season and low expectations from the press, we felt good about our chances when we left Arizona to start the year.

Meanwhile, over in St. Louis, Mark McGwire was being asked the same question every day: Can you break Roger Maris's record of 61 home runs in a single season?

Mark had made a run at the record in late 1997, hitting 58 home runs in a year when he was traded from the Oakland Athletics to the St. Louis Cardinals. If not for a slump that he experienced in the uncertain period just before he was traded, there were a lot of people who thought he could have broken the record, because once he got to St. Louis, he really took off.

Once he could focus on baseball and be cheered like a hero at Busch Stadium, the attention was on Mark to make a run at baseball's biggest record, which had stood since 1961. My parents hadn't even met in 1961. Mark hadn't even been born in 1961.

And there was only one Ken Griffey in the world back in

1961—and he was still a long way from a distinguished big-league career and fathering a son who would take his name. And what a son he has! By the time 1998 rolled around, Griffey Jr. had had five 100-plus-RBI seasons. There are great players in the Baseball Hall of Fame who haven't done that. In 1997 Griffey hit 56 home runs. In 1996 he hit 49 despite spending three weeks on the disabled list. Griffey and McGwire. Those two guys were all alone in a hallowed circle.

Meanwhile, I kept working in Chicago. I had gone into the year with a new mindset, but as April progressed, my power numbers weren't there yet. I had many conversations with Jeff Pentland as we worked to find the right formula.

Jeff Pentland:

Sammy started very slowly. Around the middle of May, he had only eight home runs. I think in April he was batting around .200. The problem was that he had kind of hung on to his old ways.

So in the middle of May, we had a conversation. When you talk to Sammy, he is a cocky, confident son of a gun. He is always going to tell you that he is fine, that I should go and help some of the other guys. But I felt it was my job to say something. I'm that way with all the hitters, and certainly you're going to say something when they are struggling.

At that point, I don't think Sammy was totally sold on how he was stepping. He wasn't doing what we talked about in spring training. I felt he was still swinging too hard. I wanted to slow Sammy down. He was so aggressive and so emo-

tional—he didn't need to speed up anymore. I was asking him
to make a drastic change, and that wasn't easy for him.

But we started doing some drills where I would stand
about twenty feet away from him, with a screen in front of
me, and just throw the ball underhand to him. It's a drill de-
signed to create a good direction for your swing and to keep
it slow. I was trying to get him to wait.

Now at this point he wasn't as bad as he had been, but he
certainly wasn't where I felt he was in spring training. I think
the problem was just part of the emotion of playing the season. Sammy gets fired up. This guy really gets into it. As a
coach you love that, and I couldn't write a script for a better
player. Usually the guys like that are only five-foot-two and
weigh 140 pounds. Here I had a guy as strong as an ox, with
tremendous leg drive. But what Sammy had more than anything else was a will and an aggressiveness that I've never
seen in anybody I've ever coached. All we had to do was harness it.

As I said before, Sammy's play had made him a lot of
money. But I think Sammy wanted more than that. And so he
changed. I give him a lot of credit. I've given the same coaching tips to fifty or a hundred other guys, but Sammy was the
one who listened and was able to make the adjustments. Obviously, he is someone special.

The key was that I understood him as a person. As a
coach, if you just understand Sammy from a technical
standpoint, then you're missing most of the person. I
wouldn't say he's insecure, but there are always some inner
questions that Sammy has. These are questions I think we
all battle. I understood that when Sammy wasn't doing
well, he was hurting. So after we had our conversation, we
agreed that we were going to make a total commitment to
the program we were doing. And Sammy agreed. And then
he took off.

Sammy:

Jeff Pentland is a hitting instructor who has helped me in every way. He is an excellent person. Of all the coaches I've had in my life, he is the one who has gotten the most out of me. He is the one who understands me.

Jeff Pentland:

Sammy started hitting the cover off the ball, but into May he hadn't really hit that many home runs. He was hitting balls so hard they were hitting the brick wall at Wrigley Field and bouncing back to the infield. He wasn't getting the ball elevated. In fact, he came over to me at one point and said that he loved what he was doing but was hoping he would hit a few more home runs. I realized there were home runs built into Sammy's body, but it was something I never worried about. I was more concerned with his plate coverage, his ability to cover the ball away and the ball in.

After a while, he fell in love with what he was learning—he fell in love with his ability to drive the baseball to right field harder than anybody in the game. When you do something well, you tend to want to do it some more. That's what happened. And once he did that—nobody in baseball could touch him.

Sammy:

When things started to roll for me, I did my work calmly, keeping an even keel. And once I started, I didn't stop. The home runs came like rain. . . .

June 1998

Sammy:

People remember the month of June as the month I hit more home runs than any player in the history of baseball. But truth be told, the streak started in late May, in the most unlikely of places—Atlanta.

Throughout my career Braves pitching has been tough on me, as it has been for everybody else. And going into that series, I was nowhere near Mark McGwire or any of the other league leaders in home runs.

When we arrived in Georgia, I had only eight home runs through the first six weeks of the season.

And not only were we in Atlanta, but we were facing Greg Maddux himself. It was May 22. Everybody knows that Greg Maddux and I were teammates for one year in 1992. It was his last year with the Cubs and my first. He's a good guy and he was a good teammate. And of course, he's a great pitcher who's always been a challenge for me. But in what would be a special year, I began it all by hitting a 440-foot shot off a special pitcher. It happened in the first inning, when I hit one of Maddux's pitches to straight center.

I had home run number 9.

Before that homer off of Maddux, I had hit home runs here and there. But everything was different from then on.

As Jeff said, by relaxing at the plate and shifting my weight to my back leg, I was starting to connect to right field. That made me even more dangerous as a hitter because I was now crushing pitches that were off the plate—pitches I used to miss.

Three days later, against Braves pitcher Kevin Millwood, I

hit number 10. This one was to right field—410 feet. Four innings later, with two runners on base, I hit a 420-foot shot to straight-away center field against Millwood's reliever, Michael Cather. Number 11. And the chase was on.

On May 27 I hit two home runs against the Phillies, numbers 12 and 13. On June 1, we were home against the Florida Marlins: two home runs, 14 and 15. I then hit one on June 3. I hit another on June 5, against the White Sox. And another against the Sox on June 6. And yet another against the Sox on June 7, capping a thrilling three-game sweep of my former team by scores of 6–5, 7–6, and 13–7. Then there was another homer against the Twins on June 8. Suddenly, I had 20 home runs. But I still wasn't drawing much national attention. It didn't matter, though. I had never felt so good in my career. It didn't matter to me who was pitching. I felt so confident.

On June 13 it started again in Philadelphia.

We were facing Mark Portugal, the pitcher the White Sox once considered swapping for me until the Houston Astros decided against it. I hit a two-run shot to right field, number 21.

Two days later, we were home against the Milwaukee Brewers and Cal Eldred. I hit three off of Cal. In the first inning, I hit number 22 right field; in the third inning, I hit 23 to left field; and in the seventh inning, I hit 24 to center field. On June 17, still at Wrigley against the Brewers, I hit another one, number 25.

Then the Phillies came to town. On June 19, I hit two, 26 and 27. On June 20, I hit two more, 28 and 29, the latter a 500-foot bomb to left that was my longest home run of the season. And on June 21, I hit another, a solo shot to right field off Tyler Green.

I had 30 home runs, and it was only June 21.

And I had 17 home runs for the month, a mark putting me in exclusive company: I had tied the National League record held by the great Willie Mays, who hit 17 in August of 1965.

The major-league record had been set by Rudy York of the Detroit Tigers, who hit 18 in August 1937. So it was only fitting that I hit number 18 at Tiger Stadium, in an interleague game on June 24. And then the next day, still in Detroit, I broke the record with a 400-foot shot to right field off of Brian Moehler.

It seemed like that would be it, the record would stand at 19. But in my last at-bat, on the last game of the month—a home game against the Arizona Diamondbacks, on June 30—I hit a solo home run off of Alan Embree, number 20 for the month of June and number 33 overall.

At the end of June, the All-Star ballots were counted, with Mark McGwire getting the most votes of any player by far. I didn't even finish in the top ten in the voting. In the National League outfield, Tony Gwynn, Barry Bonds, Larry Walker, Dante Bichette, and Moises Alou finished ahead of me in the balloting.

America was just getting to know me.

A Summer to Remember

It didn't matter to me that I didn't get voted onto the starting lineup of the All-Star Game by the fans. I knew that if I kept going, people would eventually appreciate me. When I was younger, I didn't have the perspective that I have now. Back then, I would do things I shouldn't have done. I wanted everything all at once.

But I knew by the midway point of the 1998 season that I had finally found the discipline I needed to excel in this game.

You want to know what I was really thinking of at that point? I was thanking God for all that I had been through. It had made me a better person and a better player. And now I would go out and show it. Besides, I was picked to the All-Star team as a reserve. I was thrilled and traveled to Denver for the game, even though I had a slight injury that kept me from playing. But I went anyway. I just felt good being there, and I had a great time talking to the fans and being around people.

At last, amazing things were starting to happen, and I was ready for them. I had the wisdom of my years in baseball and the wisdom of lessons my mother and family taught me as a child. In 1998, all of those things came together for me.

But the fact that I was achieving great things made me feel humble.

Remember when I was fifteen and about to sign a contract with the Phillies, when my brother and I were haggling for more money but my mother felt uncomfortable with the whole thing? When I told her we could have gotten more money from the Phillies, she said, "No son, don't think that way. Be satisfied with what God gives you." She was right, and I decided, in the summer of 1998, that I would keep trying to get the most out of my potential—and then be satisfied with whatever came my way.

It was that principle that I followed every time someone would ask me about Mark McGwire. From mid to late July, people were asking me about him a lot. During the first part of 1998, as I said earlier, Mark and Ken Griffey Jr. were in a hallowed circle all by themselves. What I did that summer was enter into that circle even though I hadn't been invited. And as time went on, people wanted to know if I was upset that Mark and Ken were getting more attention than I was. The answer to that question is simple. No.

But as much as I tried to ignore it or make jokes about it, the questions kept coming, especially after *Time* magazine did a cover story on the home-run race in late July and put only Mark and Ken on the cover. Inside there was a story about me that read, in part, "Sosa is the dark-horse candidate to shatter the single-season record for home runs. Thanks to a spectacular—some might say freaky—June in which he popped 20 home runs, a major-league record, the Dominican native showed that he is finally harnessing his impulsiveness."

The headline on that story read, "Hey Guys, Watch Your Backs—Here Comes Sammy!"

But while the home-run chase was just heating up, something much more important was happening: the Cubs were fighting for a playoff spot. After our horrible finish in 1997, we were in the hunt after the All-Star break.

By this point, the people of Chicago were mine. And my blown-kiss salute to Mama became famous. To me, that is the most important, most meaningful thing that happened in 1998, that the whole world learned of my love for my mother. With each home run the cameras would flash on me in the dugout, poised for me to blow a kiss, and I never let them down. And if anybody thinks that my mother is not watching or not expecting her kiss after each and every home run, they should think again. She always watches, and she always looks for it. Always.

By 1998 she was living in a lovely home I had bought for her in San Pedro de Macorís, and she could watch all the games from the comfort of her living room. She was starting to get attention. Reporters were starting to seek her out, to find out about the life she had given my brothers, sisters, and me. That made me happy because she deserved every accolade in the world.

On July 28 I blew kiss number 41 to Mama after hitting a homer against the Diamondbacks in Phoenix. With two months to go, I had passed my own milestone by surpassing the 40 home runs I hit in the injury-shortened season of 1996. I finished July with 42 home runs.

On August 5, I hit number 43 off Arizona's Andy Benes at Wrigley. On August 8, against the Cardinals in St. Louis in the ninth inning, I hit number 44 by launching a 400-foot homer into the left-field stands at Busch Stadium. That put us ahead, but we lost that game in a heartbreaker in the bottom of the ninth.

On August 10, at Candlestick Park in San Francisco, I hit numbers 45 and 46—the second one a 480-foot shot to straight center, one of my longest home runs of the season.

Then, on August 16, at the Houston Astrodome, I hit number 47, a solo shot that was the margin of victory in a 2–1 win. That was a big win because we were chasing the Astros for the lead in the National League Central Division.

More than any home runs or accolades, I wanted to reach the playoffs—I had never been to the postseason. Other players had told me about playing in that atmosphere, and I wanted to experience it, to play for the ultimate prize in our game.

So by August every game counted. And one contest that really stands out in my mind was a game we played on August 19. We were at home in Wrigley, facing the St. Louis Cardinals. Going into the game, Mark and I were tied with 47 home runs each, with six weeks to go in the season. By the time this game rolled around, the media attention was incredible. There was a crush of television camera crews, and it seemed like what Mark and I were doing was taking on a larger meaning. People were focused on baseball again after all the negativity from the strike.

Meanwhile, reporters kept asking me: "Do you feel slighted that Mark McGwire is getting more attention than you are?" Newspapers were writing about us and saying things like, "The home-run chase in black and white."

In that type of atmosphere, Mark and I put on a show on August 19. I hit number 48 to take the lead briefly. Then

Mark hit numbers 48 and 49. At one point late in the game, I drew a walk and trotted down to first base. Mark was standing there, and—to my surprise—he imitated the kisses I blew to Mama and patted me on the back. It was a nice gesture. People have asked me what we said to each other at that moment, when all the cameras were trained on us and we were the center of the baseball world. I don't remember his exact words, but it was something like, "Hey, I think we're going to do it." It was an acknowledgment that Roger Maris's record was within reach. After the game—for the first time—Mark told the press that he thought the record was breakable.

I wasn't disappointed that Mark had caught me and passed me in my home ballpark. I was disappointed that we had lost the game, but in baseball, you have to put yesterday behind and concentrate on tomorrow. The San Francisco Giants were coming to town, and they were shaping up to be our competition for the wild-card spot in the playoffs. On August 21 I hit home run number 49, a two-run blast off Orel Hersheiser that helped beat the Giants at Wrigley, 6–5. Two days later, still at Wrigley, we faced the Houston Astros again. It was during that game that one of the stranger events of 1998 happened to me. I hit two home runs off of Jose Lima, who went on to a 21-win season in 1999. But after the game, when I expected to talk about my home runs number 50 and 51, people asked if Lima had "grooved" some easy pitches to me to hit. The suspicion was that Lima, being my countryman and possessing a big lead that day, had lobbed a few easy pitches to me so I could pad my stats. I couldn't believe my ears. What an insulting thought to even suggest.

Let me say this so there is no confusion: in this league, nobody "grooves" anything. You can either play the game or you can't. Lima pitched to me, and I hit the ball. Nobody gave anything away. It was late August, after all, and every team still in the hunt was fighting for every game.

This particular situation was an example of how the national attention focused on Mark and me was taking different forms every day.

For example, by late summer, Mark was answering lots of questions about his use of Androstenedione, a muscle-building hormone. The implication was that Andro pills were helping feed his home-run prowess. Making it an even more delicate situation, people were asking me about Mark's Andro use as well—I suppose because he and I were linked so closely by this point.

What I said then is what I say today: What Mark does is none of my business.

I can only speak for myself. And I have never used Andro, nor do I plan to. By 1998, my upper body had developed significantly from my first year in the majors, when I was a skinny twenty-year-old from San Pedro. While it's true that I tried the food supplement Creatine once or twice, I never saw it have any particular impact on my body or development. The truth is, I attribute my physical development to many years of strict weight training and proper nutrition.

Old friends like Larry Himes saw firsthand how much my body developed from 1989 into the early 1990s. Frankly, a lot of my growth came from eating well after a malnourished childhood. The same can be said for a lot of Latin players. You can always tell when one of us has spent time in the States: when we go home we stand out among our skinny friends.

Before the month of August was over, I hit four more home runs—on August 26, 28, 30, and 31.

A Historic September

I had 55 going into September and would hit three more between September 2 and September 5, which gave me 58.

Number 57 was historic because it broke Hack Wilson's single-season record for most home runs by a Cub—a record that had stood since 1930. That came in Pittsburgh. Then we went to St. Louis and witnessed Mark pass Roger Maris's record. It was an incredible evening—a media crush that outdid everything we had seen in the weeks before. And that is saying a lot.

Going into the game, I had never seen Mark so focused. And after he hit number 62, I had never seen him so happy. I was deeply touched when he acknowledged me to the crowd. Everyone remembers our embrace at midfield. Mark was happy, and I was happy for him. I've often been asked why I was so happy for Mark and why I kept calling him "the man." For me it was just a way of showing my respect and admiration for him. Mark is a truly great player. But more important than that, Mark is a good person, a far more important quality than hitting home runs.

Since that year he and I have talked several times. We've gone out to dinner, and we've shared some really nice moments as friends.

Jeff Pentland:

More than anything else, I was proud of the way Sammy went about his business. He was so classy. He was under so much pressure, and still he maintained his approach. No matter how hectic things got, he prepared for games the same way every day. He was never overly nervous or excited, and he maintained his demeanor and openness to people. Good players just elevate their game, and that's what he did.

After McGwire broke the record, Sammy was a little down—I could tell. He would never say anything, but I knew him so well. And when I saw McGwire, it looked like a hundred tons had been lifted off his shoulders. It was like "Wow, it's over."

As a coach you try to use whatever you can to motivate somebody. So I said to Sammy, "You know what? I think you're going to go out there and pound the ball and you're going to get right back in this thing."

Sammy:

Jeff was right. On September 11, at home at Wrigley, I hit number 59 against the Milwaukee Brewers. Then the next day, in the seventh inning of a game we won 15–12 against the Brewers, I hit a three-run home run, number 60.

Jeff Pentland:

At that point I got very teary-eyed. I had to go back in the tunnel on the way to the clubhouse because my emotions just overcame me. In my mind, 60 had always been a magical number, and at that moment everything just kind of hit me.

After a while, I just couldn't hold back my tears, and I just lost it. Who was I? Where did I come from? I was a nobody, and here I was a part of history. It was overwhelming to me.

Sammy:

The next day was the ultimate for me. In the fifth inning against the Brewers, while facing Bronswell Patrick, I hit a two-run homer, number 61. I had passed the great Babe Ruth. I had equaled the previous record of Roger Maris. And I had pulled to within one home run of my friend Mark. The emotions were welling inside of me, but we still had a game to finish, and we were in a tight struggle.

I came up in the ninth. We were behind. I was facing Eric Plunk.

Home run number 62.

It's hard to describe the emotions I was feeling as I ran around the bases. I had wanted this so much, and now I had achieved it. Everything had come to me, everything I had ever dreamed of, and now I was rounding the bases as a part of history.

We won the game 11–10, and afterward the crowd gave me an ovation that will remain in my heart forever. I was very emotional as I acknowledged the crowd, and afterward the full force of what I had done hit me. There were still two weeks to go in the season, and we were fighting for our lives in the Central Division.

My name was now a part of history, and suddenly—as if we hadn't been in the limelight already—the media turned up the heat even more. By the time we got to San Diego after the Milwaukee series, an army of reporters was waiting for me.

The first day we had to have a press conference before the game in a separate locker room to accommodate the media. Everywhere I went, people trailed after me. All the television networks were following me, as were the major newspapers and magazines. I was on the cover of *Sports Illustrated*. ESPN did a whole hour with me. Reporters were getting on airplanes and flying to the Dominican Republic to see my roots for themselves.

I just took it all in. And I can truly say that I enjoyed it. The crowds didn't bother me; the media didn't bother me. I was focused on what I had to do, and nothing was going to stand in my way.

By that San Diego series, capacity crowds were standing and cheering every time I came up to the plate—and I was a visiting player! For the first two games of that series, I hadn't come close to connecting, but in the third game, on September 16, I came up to bat in the top of the eighth with the bases loaded. We were losing 3–2 to an extremely talented Padres team that later ended up in the World Series that year.

Brian Boehringer was pitching when I connected. The ball sailed into the second deck of the left-field bleachers, and the crowd cheered as if I played for the Padres—number 63. The Padres set off fireworks as I rounded the bases. The Cubs went on to win the game 6–3, with me driving in all six runs. I was inside the dugout, taking congratulations, when the San Diego crowd made me take a curtain call. What a thrill! Afterward so many reporters and camera crews jammed into our clubhouse that several of my teammates couldn't get to their lockers.

But I was disappointed to hear later that some Padres players had reacted angrily to the fireworks that were set off after my home run. To me, there was no reason for those players to react that way. More than anything else, it seemed like an act of jealousy. What people were responding to was history.

The main thing was that baseball was popular again, people were going to the games, and they weren't talking about the strike anymore. I'm proud to look back and know that Mark and I played a role in that revival. People really got behind us. And to me that season proved that you can excel and you can win and you can still be happy for someone else.

I hit three more home runs before the season was over and, as everyone knows, Mark finished with 70 home runs to my 66.

Most important, I was thrilled that we reached the National League playoffs. And even though it didn't go well for us against Atlanta, when the season was finally over, the fans reached out to me, and I ran around Wrigley Field to thank them for everything. I felt it was a fitting way to cap off a wondrous season—I wanted the fans at Wrigley to share in my joy.

My numbers for that season are now well known: .308 batting average, 66 home runs, and a major-league-leading 158 RBI. I also led the league in runs scored with 134. I won the National League MVP trophy.

The Dominican community of New York threw a parade for me in the streets of that beautiful city. And I returned home to my country a national hero. When I got there, the countryside had been badly damaged by Hurricane Georges—and it was then that I decided to start my foundation. The goal of my foundation was and is to help people in need in my country. How could I not?

When I arrived home, people lined the streets. You could still see the damage from the hurricane, and it rained very, very hard—but still the people were there by the thousands. It touched my heart to see them all, to know they had waited for me in the rain. I'll never forget that day.

The whole year had been like a dream for me, one where all of my hopes and aspirations came true. And though I had faced so much scrutiny, I didn't plan on running away. I wanted to experience all there was to my new life. I wanted to see it all. So I prepared myself for a busy winter. I thanked God for my blessings. I truly relished my life.

12

Sammy Sosa

The memories of 1998 are truly incredible, and they play in my mind like a favorite movie. It's just hard to believe that this movie is about me. One scene that is a favorite is the Sammy Sosa Day celebration the Cubs held in my honor late in the 1998 season. I'll never forget my emotional pride at seeing the Dominican flag flying in the center-field stands at Wrigley. My mother and my whole family were there—which was so beautiful. That was one day where I could really say, *"Wow!"*

Another favorite memory: the night we beat the San Francisco Giants in a one-game playoff that put us in the postseason—a first for me. When we won, I was there on top of the dugout, dancing my merengue. When the year was over, the invitations began flooding in. I was on the *Tonight Show* with Jay Leno, and on the *Late Show* with David Letterman. I then returned to Chicago at the invitation of the mayor.

When I got home to the Dominican, the president of my country—the honorable Leonel Fernandez—made me an ambassador. With that distinction my family and I were given special passports that allowed us to travel all over the world.

And I used that privilege to promote my country, my beautiful island nation.

There was so much to do when I got home because there was so much devastation after Hurricane Georges. It was a horrible catastrophe, a storm that destroyed much of the countryside. I was proud to use my name to help bring water, food, clothing, and everything that was necessary to the people who needed it.

Particularly hurt were the poorest of my nation, people living in outlying areas where there was no protection from the pounding rain and wind. When I saw the damage, my heart sank because I knew the plight of all those people. Most touching of all was the sight of people in my hometown of San Pedro, cheering me amid all the rubble and downed trees and power lines.

The press said there were a half-million people lining the streets to greet me. When I traveled to the United States during that off-season, I tried my best to raise money for hurricane relief. My foundation opened the Sammy Sosa Children's Medical Center for Preventative Medicine in San Pedro de Macorís. We opened it with the generous help of the Centers for Disease Control and Prevention in Atlanta, the U.S. government, and the government of my country. Today my clinic gives free immunizations to children in the five provinces surrounding San Pedro de Macorís.

Opening the clinic was a great source of pride. And though I didn't open it for recognition, I was deeply honored when Major League Baseball bestowed on me the Roberto Clemente Man of the Year Award. To receive an award named after Clemente was something I'll never forget.

Meanwhile, the invitations kept coming in. I went to Japan and played in several exhibition games before wildly enthusiastic fans. I fed off their energy, and in 24 at-bats, I got 12

hits—a .500 average—with 3 homers and 9 RBI, earning me
MVP honors on a team of major-league all-stars.

I was then invited to the White House to light the national Christmas tree. I met the leaders of Puerto Rico in
San Juan. While there, I paid homage to the great Clemente.

I went to the ESPY Awards, where I was presented with a
Humanitarian Award. I then flew to Los Angeles for a photo
shoot with Mark McGwire. We had been named "Sportsmen
of the Year" by *Sports Illustrated*. We earned the same honor
from the *Sporting News,* which had also named me Player of
the Year. I was given similar honors by *Baseball Weekly* and
Baseball Digest and was selected as the Players Choice Man
of the Year.

Through the holidays and into 1999, I was living on airplanes. I swear, I was flying every two days. My manager,
Domingo, and I were fielding numerous offers for endorse-
ments. And soon I was filming countless commercials.

President Clinton invited me back to Washington as his
guest at the State of the Union address. I sat with the First
Lady and was honored when the president singled me out for
applause. Here I was, once a humble kid from the Dominican, and now the lawmakers of the United States were standing and applauding me in the halls of Congress. It was a great
moment.

President Clinton couldn't have been nicer to me. He is
the leader of the free world, but on a human level, because of
his kindness toward my family and me, I consider him a
friend.

But after a while I think my fans began getting worried
that I wasn't going to have a good season in 1999. Some said
I was traveling too much. I wasn't worried. I knew that I was
taking care of myself. I was getting my rest. I was eating
well. And despite the hectic schedule, my baseball prepara-

tion did not suffer. My life just got busier. I was doing my work while meeting a lot of people known the world over. One after the other, I met Donald Trump, Danny Glover, Denzel Washington, Jennifer Lopez, Oscar de la Renta, Gloria and Emilio Estefan. My favorite movie is *Titanic*, and I was happy to meet its star, Leonardo DiCaprio. I got to know Oprah. While I was in New York, I met Cardinal O'Connor and Mayor Rudy Giuliani. And I was honored to meet the Rev. Jesse Jackson.

But while it was all fun and those months provided a lifetime of memories, I never lost focus. And when I arrived in Mesa, Arizona, for spring training in February 1999, I was ready to work. I knew I could do my job because I had done it under the kind of media scrutiny that only one other player knew as well as me—Mark McGwire. He had done his job in the summer and fall of 1998, and so had I. The night I hit the grand slam in San Diego, I had been able to focus while a capacity crowd stood and roared every time I stepped up to the plate. Meanwhile, the press corps got bigger and bigger.

I am very single-minded, and I just concentrate harder so I can handle those situations. I knew I could do it again in 1999.

Jeff Pentland:

It was incredible to watch Sammy because you saw the transformation of a person. What's more important than Sammy's success on the field is how he has grown emotionally. His physical skill was a big thing, no question, but the most important thing was the person he became. He just doesn't let little things bother him—he is so far past that stuff.

Let's put it this way: Sammy doesn't have a lot of distractions. I mean, obviously, he has them, but he doesn't allow them to create a problem. His priority is to be the best player he can be. Other than his family and his religion, nothing comes before that.

And he fed off of what was happening to him in 1998. It was his life. It was his food. He was consumed by it. He went through his peaks and valleys, but then we would talk, and you would watch him go out and use what we had talked about. It was incredible.

When I look back on 1998, one of the moments that made me feel great was when the Cleveland Indians came to town. This was after Sammy had hit the 20 home runs in June. During batting practice before one game, Sammy stepped into the cage, and suddenly there must have been fifteen players from the Indians all hovering around watching. I mean, Cleveland has a great offensive ball club, and here was Manny Ramirez and all these other great Dominican hitters standing around making really positive comments about Sammy. They were saying how much he had changed, how his technique was better, how his swing was more under control.

Looking back now, I think that getting the full respect of the other Dominican players was the ultimate for Sammy. Afterward, Manny Ramirez and some of the others said some really nice things to Sammy. And some even came over and patted me on the back. That's why you coach. Not for the money, but for moments like that.

But Sammy doesn't need my help anymore. He's there. He's learned a great deal about himself and a great deal about hitting in general. By 1999 I would see him making more comments about other players and their hitting. I think he's got the confidence now, and other players are coming to him. He is much more in a leadership role.

Sammy:

Going into spring training in 1999, there were lots of questions about Mark and me. Mark said that 1998 couldn't happen again. But I said, "Why not?" And I started hitting home runs in spring training.

But I started the season slowly. I was playing my game, but people were saying I would have a letdown. But I always thought, it's not how I begin a season, it's how I end it. And through April, I had only four home runs. But then, in May, I hit 13. For that month I also hit .321 with 27 RBI and 26 runs scored, earning National League Player of the Month honors for the third time in my career.

Then, in June, I hit another 13 home runs. At the start of July, I was sitting on 30 home runs again, which made me very proud. And after a decade in the game, the fans voted me to the starting lineup of the All-Star Game for the first time. I was thrilled to be the top vote-getter in baseball, with 2.3 million votes.

At that game in Boston, I faced my countryman Pedro Martinez. I had seen him in the National League when he was with the Expos, but this time was different. He had a great curveball and great command—just incredible. He may be the best pitcher I've ever faced in my career. And being around the other all-stars was a thrill because I had the respect of my peers.

Jeff Pentland:

To me what was so great about 1999 was that Sammy was now consistently hitting the best pitchers in the game. That was huge. Now he was able to hit well against Randy Johnson,

Kevin Brown, Curt Schilling. You could go down the list, and Sammy hit off them—that was special.

And what you have to realize was that as a team, the Cubs had such a bad year in 1999 that we almost never faced the middle pitchers—who are the worst pitchers in the game.

We were always facing starters, setup guys, and closers. But that didn't affect Sammy. As a hitting purist, I loved the fact that he was not only hitting home runs but had also raised his batting average. His ability to drive in runs with men on base is great. And he's becoming a tremendous two-strike hitter.

Sammy:

I hit 10 home runs in July to raise my total to 40 going into August. Mark was hitting home runs just as he had the year before as well. But the country wasn't captivated the way it had been in 1998 because it was the second time around for us. Plus, we were suffering through a horrible season in Chicago. All the hope of 1998 faded to a season reminiscent of 1997 and 1994. To begin with, Kerry Wood—our rookie sensation from the year before—hurt his arm and missed the entire season.

We suffered other injuries, and we just didn't play well. Everything seemed to go wrong for us as a team. And when it was over, we had lost 95 games—one more loss than our horrible season of 1997. That was very tough to take because after making the playoffs the year before, we wanted to experience that again.

Into August we were losing as a team, but I was still hitting home runs—a total of 15 for the month. That was the most I hit in any month of the season. I felt so confident at the plate and was so convinced in what I was doing. I hit home runs on

August 2 and August 4. Then I hit one on August 9 and one on August 14, two on August 15, one on August 16, two more on August 20, two more on August 21, one on August 25, another on August 26, and one each on August 29 and August 31.

Going into September, I had 55 home runs.

Jeff Pentland:

I think Sammy had a better year in 1999 than he did in 1998. Particularly with what was going on with the Cubs. For us as a team, 1999 was a lot worse than 1997. In 1997 we didn't have the talent—we had some guys who probably shouldn't have been there. It was just a bad Cubs team. In 1999 we certainly were a bad team, but with the talent we had we should have been a lot better than we were. So what you get is a bad taste in your mouth. You get a clubhouse that isn't any good. You get players nitpicking each other. The atmosphere just affects everyone. It's difficult to play under those circumstances.

So I give Sammy an enormous amount of credit for playing the way he did—what he did was monumental.

Sammy:

With my friend Michael Jordan having retired, some people began to say I was the biggest star in Chicago sports. To tell the truth, it's not something I think about. I would never go around saying, "Yeah, I'm the star." It's not my nature to go around pronouncing things. If people are going to say nice things, I will take their words thankfully. But I'm going to continue to try and be a humble person because I want kids to see that. That's important to me.

But let me get back to the last month of the season. I hit 8 home runs in September, finishing with 63. When I hit number 60 off of Jason Bere of the Milwaukee Brewers at Wrigley Field, I became the first player in major-league history to have back-to-back 60-homer years. Then Mark McGwire reached 60 as well and finished the season with 65 home runs. Both of us surpassed Ruth and Maris again, and what made me happiest was that I hit number 63 in St. Louis while the president of the Dominican Republic was present.

People have often asked me if I was upset that Mark ultimately hit more home runs than I did by the end of the season. The answer is no. I didn't feel bad. I felt proud of what I accomplished in 1999. And besides, I'm not a jealous person—I don't envy anyone. Mark deserves everything he has gotten, and I would never feel jealous of him. Maybe someday I'll win the home-run title—I certainly hope so.

Jeff Pentland:

Sammy stubbed his toe a little bit toward the end, but I think part of that was that we were so bad. But it's totally understandable because we were playing so poorly. It was probably one of the worst experiences I've ever gone through.

Sammy:

I was disappointed in our play in 1999. It was a bad year, though one bright spot was being selected to the Cubs' all-century team at the end of the season. After the season Jim Riggleman was fired as the manager and the Cubs hired Don Baylor to replace him. News of that came when I was already back in the Dominican Republic.

This off-season has been different from the last. Though the requests keep coming in, I've tried to keep my commitments to a minimum. Instead, I have concentrated on my foundation, which continues to serve the needy of my country. And I grew excited as construction of my new house neared a conclusion.

On November 12, to celebrate my thirty-first birthday, I threw a big party, a kind of housewarming for the place where my family and I will live the rest of our lives. I really wanted it to be a big party and a celebration of the previous two years.

Donald Trump flew in for it. So did the Rev. Jesse Jackson. President Fernandez was there as well, as was Julio Maria Sanguinetti, the president of Uruguay. My entire country celebrated. I'm only sorry I couldn't have invited them all to my home.

On Christmas Day I was where I am every single year—at my mother's house with the rest of my family. And, on New Year's Eve, we rang in the millennium with her.

By January 2000, I was working hard again, getting ready for the coming season. I have high hopes that the Cubs will do everything to try to win, because that's what I want most of all. I hope they will do all they can to assemble a winner in 2000 and beyond.

For my part I intend to be ready for battle, as I always am. Through January and into February, I was making three trips a week to San Pedro de Macorís to train with my people and get ready for the season. Every time I go, I love seeing old friends like Hector Peguero, who saw me take my first steps in the game of baseball.

Hector Peguero:

With each season I am there with him every step of the way. I feel that way because I've known him for so long, and despite all of his fame, he hasn't changed as a person. He still comes to see us, and when I talk to him, he's like he's always been. He's still Mikey.

And so when he is in Chicago hitting home runs, I feel like I'm hitting home runs. When he got to 63 in 1999 and people would ask me about him, I would say, I have 63 home runs.

Omar Minaya:

I think what I'm proudest of when I see Sammy is that, as a Hispanic person, I see him as such a good example, such a role model. I was in Washington, D.C., recently, in the halls of Congress, and I remember looking around and thinking, "My God, Sammy Sosa was here, and the president had him stand up and take a bow."

And then they threw that big parade for him in New York. How many times has that happened? How many times have Americans embraced someone from a foreign country in that way? I can only think of one other, and that's Nelson Mandela.

Luis Sosa:

We, as a family, are always with Sammy. He is never alone. My heart fills with pride for what he has done because I remember that young boy who I showed how to play baseball. I showed him how to throw by throwing rocks.

Now, when I see all his success, I get very emotional.

Jeff Pentland:

Because of the way he's handled himself and the great things he's done, I think Sammy certainly is to Chicago what the late Walter Payton was and Michael Jordan is. I think Sammy is right up there with them.

Mireya Sosa:

To me Sammy is the same as he's always been. And while I'm proud of what he has done as a player, I'm more proud that he is such a good son, brother, husband, and father. He's always kept me close to his heart, and he'll always be close to mine.

Sammy:

Why do I go back to San Pedro de Macorís? To be with my people. That's the most beautiful thing I have. I could never envision a time when I would be separated from them, because even once you've attained things in life, you can never leave behind who you are.

I love to be around my people. They are the people who respect me, care for me, and have always been there for me. I have all this fame now, but I will never forget where I came from.

I have so many people to thank, so much gratitude for all that I have. My life has been an incredible journey, one filled with love. I'm grateful to the city of Chicago, the Chicago Cubs, and all the wonderful people at Wrigley Field, whom I love so much. I am grateful to Larry Himes, Omar Minaya, Amado Dinzey, and Jeff Pentland for believing in me.

I am also grateful for the progress that we Latin players have made in baseball in recent years. We have overcome a lot, and I was thrilled to see Tony Perez and, before him, Orlando Cepeda inducted into the Baseball Hall of Fame. Maybe someday I'll be in the Hall of Fame myself. That is the dream of all ballplayers.

In the meantime, I owe so much to Mr. and Mrs. Bill Chase for being there for me. To my best friend, Domingo Dauhajre, his wife, Yanilka, and their beautiful family. To my beautiful wife, Sonia, and my children. And to my brothers and sisters.

But most of all I would like to say thank you to the person who gave me life—the one who is responsible for what I am today. Whenever I think of her, my eyes well up, and my heart fills with love. Because of her, I have everything. And because of her example, which I use as my guide, the world has opened to me in ways I could have never imagined.

So, in the 2000 season, with each home run, I'll keep doing what I've always done—I'll keep blowing kisses to her. It's the least I can do, and it's a symbol of how much she means to me. So to finish this story for now, I will say what is in my heart and what I think after each and every home run: "I love you, Mama."

Thank you.

Author's Note

This book was primarily told through the words of Sammy Sosa and the most important people in his life. But the author also wishes to thank the magnificent sports staff at the *Chicago Tribune*, whose coverage of Sammy Sosa since 1989 has added weight, perspective, and context to the recollections of Mr. Sosa and others quoted in this book. In addition, articles from the *Sporting News, Sports Illustrated*, the *Dallas Morning News*, and Associated Press were used to corroborate dates, games, and statistics, as was the official Chicago Cubs Web site. All interviews with Sammy Sosa were conducted in Spanish and translated into English.

Acknowledgments

I would like to thank the following people: Domingo Dauhajre; Jeff Pentland, the Cubs' hitting coach; Lou Weisbach of Ha-Lo; Marc Perman and Matt Bialer of the William Morris Agency; and Dr. Yanilka Morales.

Sammy Sosa
March 2000

I owe a debt of gratitude to my editor, Rick Wolff, for giving me the opportunity to do this book and for his kindness, generosity, and skill. Thanks also to the best literary agent working: Peter Sawyer of the Fifi Oscard Agency. Many, many thanks to Bill Chase, Larry Himes, Omar Minaya, Hector Peguero, Amado Dinzey, and Jeff Pentland for sharing their time and the stories that were so valuable to this book.

In the Dominican Republic, I am indebted to Mario Peña, my MVP on the island. Thank you to Mireya Sosa, Luis Sosa, Domingo Dauhajre, and Judy Corletto. Thanks to James Meier and Steve Gietschier of the *Sporting News* and to Dan Ambrosio. Thanks also to my great friend José Luis Villegas. And to Josh du Lac and John Trotter.

Also to my editors at the *Sacramento Bee:* Rick Rodriguez, Mort Saltzman, Tom Negrete, Joyce Terhaar, and Bill Endicott. And last but not least, thanks to my family: my father, Reynaldo Bretón; my brother, Rod, and his wife, Nina; and to my in-laws, Allen and Mamie Wong and Erwin and Lisa Wong.

This book, like everything else I do, is a tribute to the memory of my mother, Elodia Bretón Martinez. As Sammy Sosa would say: "I love you, Mama."

Marcos Bretón
February 2000
Sacramento, California